THE BEAUTIFUL

# THE BEAUTIFUL

## COLLECTED POEMS

## MICHELLE TEA

MANIC D PRESS
SAN FRANCISCO

Cover Design: Scott Idleman/Blink
Production: Wendy Shimamura, Jemma Lloyd, Tracy Hussman.

Library of Congress Catologing-in-Publication Data

Tea, Michelle
    The Beautiful: Collected Poems / Michelle Tea - 1st ed.
        p. cm.
    ISBN 0-916397-89-0 (alk. paper)
        1. Lesbians -- Poetry. 2. San Francisco (Calif.) -- Poetry. I.
Title.

PS3570.E15B43 2003
811'.6--dc22

                                            2003021964

# CONTENTS

## I. THE BEAUTIFUL

## II.   OPPRESS ME BEFORE I KILL AGAIN

## III. TRIPPING ON LABIA

## IV. HEARTBREAK CIGARETTES

## V. THE CITY AT THE END OF THE WORLD

*For David West*

# THE BEAUTIFUL

unpublished poems
1993-1997

# THE BEAUTIFUL

a coke and a smoke
as we roam the grey prairie.
what sentiment do i want
to express at the end
of our world,
a terrific excitement
as we prepare
to exit
america.
many eyes
america the
hydra
the milky stuffed
beast the roast beef
sandwich
of america.
i have no doubt we
created it.
the absent truckers
stitching the states
together, the moving
monuments
of this country.
we destroy
a little bit
of everything
we pass.
the bomb tucked
dearly
into farm land.
rest stops,
missing but
a simple bolt
of certain rage.
the wake of america
at our tail oh
we could kill it,
couldn't we.

america
what shitty parents you were.
we have to
run away
again and again
we keep
coming back
to see if you missed us
but you didn't
even know
we were gone.
we write tell-all books
about our rotten childhoods
the bad food
you fed us
-the coat-hanger
beatings
can i process
my bad relationship
with america,
can we go to
couple's counseling
can we sit down and talk about
all this
bad energy?
oh america i love you
i just want to
go on a date with you
and you won't even give me
the time of day
stuck up bitch
think you're too good for me america
i could have anyone
canada london
amsterdam
is in love with me
but it's you i want
america.
what could i do
to impress you?

i could write you
an anthem
but you have
so many
fuck you
america
you're just so
emotionally
unavailable
you act like
it's everyone else's
fault, you're a
really bad
communicator
and you have
serious
boundary issues.
i think you're
really fucked up
america
i think you've got
a lot of
problems.
i keep getting all these
hang-up calls
i know
it's you america
you better cut the shit
i'm getting a restraining
order. if america comes
within 25 feet of me
i'm throwing her ass
in jail how do you like
that america you can
dish it out
but you really can't
take it america
you're such a baby
we've been together
all these years

and you still won't let me call you
girlfriend
you act like it doesn't mean
anything.
i'm over it america
i think you're really
self-loathing
you know
i made you
what you are today
i think you forget about that
well you can just forget
about everything
america
you can just forget
the whole thing
i'm going home

## McDONALD'S

I ate the burger
because I only had
two dollars.
I had three but one
for the bus
had seven earlier
needed cigarettes
iced tea.
In the financial district
of every city
the air is made of smoke.
I want to die or
move to Boston.
All day I take typing tests,
leave that place like
America, come home
to my most ultimate
squalor, sit where the dog
or cat peed, now
I really have no money.
An empty candle frozen
with coins,
my future.

It's like the way skin
would burn
after a bullet,
hot like that
a throbbing emptiness,
skin ringing out for
ripped away red.
If I could starve myself
slowly, train myself
to need less
of everything
I could get by.

Sell the accumulation
of better times,
move to New York
answer phones whip
men organize
a labor union.

I can't work for
six dollars and I
need to have a lot
of sex.
How
did I end up with
standards of
any kind?
Demanding just too much
life, let it rip away
limbs, grow back
patience
like a starfish.
Legs shift into
another shade or
leave your hands
full of tail.

This incessant
demanding
ruins her days.
She wants only
to bring me
plates of food,
move close in
sleep, fray
the sleeve
and shoulder.

It is not noble,
peeking in on
America's makeovers,
lying with the cats.

Smoke to feel fed and
keep the candle jar fat.
It's just hard to live
without money
when you know
that some people
are rich
when you felt your
panties jingle once,
coins slipped into
the slot by a
girlish hand.

*I want to live*
*passionately*
*w/you,* on
a telephone
at a table
in a deli
in Los Angeles.

I would not see
her for several
weeks.

## AUGUST-SEPTEMBER

sash talks about the lost buses
coming down 14th street when
they should be on haight street or
market.
there's a #7 shut down and
blinking on my doorstep.
public transportation is
a mysterious underworld,
like the freemasons.
all the sweet drivers who
took my expired transfers
have been whisked away, and in their place
stone-faced meanies
who wait without grace
as i feed my crumpled dollar to the machine.
these ones are greedy, not like the
discriminating machines of the laundromat
spitting tired green tongues at my fingers.

my horoscope said Try Something Different
so i thought i would have many girlfriends
instead of the traditional one.
love is like art
you know,
don't quit your day job.
one will fuck me
in the back of her rental car
at the top of the city
the other wants coffee.

today i felt hope, finding
my heart beneath the shaky pencil
of her poetry, soft scars
on paper when she was frightened
or in love,
underlining words like a student.
i had forgot to be hopeful
my heart
it was just gone so long.

gay people are lucky because
they don't have to take marriage
seriously.
i mean, it wasn't legal.
it was a joke or maybe performance art.
in the street outside the bar
the drunk pastor intones:
in this piss and shit ...
and my heart rolls down the gutter
wrapped in potato chip bags and cigarettes
to be found one year later
pressed between pages
like a flower,
dead i guess but still pretty.

i really like my landlord.
he's always coming in and out with
plastic bags in his hands,
or Burger King.
That's Really Going To Fuck
With You When The Revolution Comes,
says keri,
but i love him because his wife is dead
and he sings johnny mathis
on his karaoke machine
when he thinks we're asleep,
wedding songs.

i hardly ever write poems for girls anymore.
usually you have to break my heart and
even then it's iffy,
but she is huge.
sitting on a splintered board
i can feel her coming
i keep my eyes on the news -
they published the unabomber manifesto -
and her teeth grip my neck.

remember when i slept with my head
in a puddle at your feet?

it was humility, or atonement.
later your ankle was a pillow and
finally you pulled me up and in my sleep i
placed your hand above my heart,
like i forgot i didn't live there
anymore.

listen, i come from pavement.
in a postcard to my mother i write
Guns And Gangs Don't Frighten Me,
But Get Me Into Nature And
I'm Terrified, bullet pops for birdsong.
you could have been a tree,
strong on the ground like that,
scratching up my back
with your branches.
can we process
the nest in my chest,
is that possible.
the eggs, smashed
wings smacking angry
on my ribs,
maybe just scared.
i mean, i've seen you in bar light,
hat dipped eyes flashing
i guess i was walking easy
on the heavy i guess
i just wanted to be the first
to go.
you said nice things and
i jumped into a bush
with a girl with a steel plate
in her head.
she said she heard voices.
i liked her for a minute.

but you on the path, in the sun,
and again, the trees, and your hand shot out
to punch my heart
*knock-knock*

i'm sorry.
here is my poetic apology
my rain puddle droplets sliding
from the grease in my hair
here is the strobe light in my chest
flashing in a strange woman's jeep as i am
rolled through farm and cornfield,
toward the barren factories
of michigan,
america.

if i got it back
if i got it to glow steady
and pulse if i got it
dark and infrared
could i
pull apart skin like
a fruit torn open
could it sit in the throne
of my body
and call to you like sound
could it beat there with you
at the tip of the world
watching
as you swallow
the planets.

## ORCA

people are shouting
but it's not my fight
as i cross the street and watch
the enormous obnoxious billboards
hanging like planets
above the used car lot.
i resent the tequila ad
encouraging the thought
that life is harsh.
catch the stranger's voice as it sails
out the window
it is not my language
so it sounds like a flute
or violin,
and the girl curves by on her bicycle.
you could be her
with long hair lifting
or you could be me
heading home.
either one is fine.

inside my roommate's room is a soft fiesta
colors strung against the glass.
that i've been an orphan so long
christmas lights
make me think
of mexican restaurants
means something
good
about my life,
it is not harsh.

on the street my roommate climbs
from a car
if she knocks on my door
she will enter my poem.
in the city parked cars
become bushes,

telephone poles trees
and the girls on their bikes
are the deer.
and what about the people
cavemen, dinosaurs.
the packs of boys in big jackets
and me in my window.
i have always been touched
by our ability to find beauty here,
anywhere.
wherever you end up.
rusting fire escapes climb like ivy
buildings shed shells of paint like fall
and the vans glide
like orca
in the street

this is my nature poem.
lucy laughs because
she doesn't know what an orca is.
my life is a poem and
i'm back in it,
lying on my roommate's bed,
green,
this would be the swamplands
stinky and wet with cat pee

the world won't stop
looking pretty tonight.
my thoughts drop lightly,
like pigeon feathers that drift
to my feet,
confirming revelations.
once the entire bird fell
from the tree
it was white, an omen
zanne said that was racist
but it wasn't the color
it was the difference,
pecking with the squat bodies
evolved to blend to city sidewalks.

i should be taking out the trash
but i can't leave the window
this inside/outside
there is a girl in this poem
the way there is smoke or air
in this room.
cryptic.
she is a mountain
she has that much
presence.
saying goodbye inside her car
she offered me her wrist.
so i bit. then kissed.
she rolled her eyes. bit again.
do it right if you're going
to do that
so i really sunk them in,
the teeth the canine ones,
pointy. and she yelped.
i didn't even care about how dorky i felt
there in the seat
i was that happy.

i don't know why i get so excited
around you.
you think it's coffee but it's not.
it's those sound waves you've been
talking about, resonance.
don't ask me how.
probably this interests no one
but me,
how hank williams faded out
and there was harsh guitar that looked
exactly like the angle of your cheek
and i shook.
it was in the cafe.
i was glad they had selected
the appropriate soundtrack
to your presence.

when i told you i dreamt
we were at disneyland
in a little car
waiting for the ride to start
i didn't realize
how much i was saying.
disneyland makes me think
of tired scared mother
but it wasn't the location,
it was the anticipated rise
to the top of the tracks
beside you and your incredible
presence.

this poem is as long as the night.
discarding the house for the bar
not even my old girlfriend
beneath the streetlight in
her fancy new clothes
can shake me.
walking with lucy
i feel such camaraderie
for the street
sash on her rattling skateboard
all my girl friends are really boys
it's our secret
the way her shirt sways
as she rides
past that fucking tequila billboard

i like to give advice
i'm good at it
tell sash to err
on the side of excess
tell roxxie to lie back,
let the universe have its way
with her.
i was afraid
i was wrong
and people do get old

tell ali it's true,
a person really can ruin
your life.
an entire life ruined,
imagine.

but it's not like that at all.
allison would like to think
it comes from me and not the girl
the way lucy thinks the same
about the aliens, or god.
all of the people
and their wonderful thoughts
how did it happen that we think,
leaning over tables,
smoking,
something inside
churning.

i want to say more,
everything.
meaningless information
like the amount of carbohydrates
in beer
could have meaning
if you're hungry.
i like my fingers
when they smell like cigarettes
rubber bands
sour metal.
pussy too.
i sniff them.

maybe i only think
this is a poem.
maybe it's a letter.
to you, silly.

## X-GIRL

i could slap at you
like a skinny mosquito
nursing my arm, the relief
of all you sucked
hitting my skin, red.

was it like that,
like food,
take what you need
shit the rest
flush
was i a burger or something?

in the kitchen that's yours now
pretending to be comfortable
and not observant so you could
pretend to be comfortable or
maybe you truly are
with your boot on the chair
and your new girl
sleek
beside you

don't say goodbye.
i swing the gate open
and get whacked by air
should've worn a jacket or
something heavy.
that life just moves
and doesn't give a fuck
what it's shifting
this is authentic time,
the part we can't grasp
free of watches
and snooze buttons
physical time
my roommate tells me
i look older now

*seasoned* she says
well it was a rough
year i said
like, shitty.
those marks,
hour hand
minute hand
circling the clock
of my face.

## SELL-OUT

how do men get away
with writing such truly
crappy poetry while i
beat my notebook
with my starving heart
here, in the mouth of my window
where you can always find me.
even david bowie
who i really do admire
crooning earnest trash
about death and youth
on my stereo
is it that simple
my old boyfriend advised me
to write romance novels,
stephen king, *you'd be rich*
he shrugged *jokes on them*
and my very own mother
tried to push me
into writing for hallmark
integrity,
like clitoris and what else,
labia, probably orgasm
it's like they were spanish words,
german, something outside our
culture.
we said parlor instead of
living room, frigging
instead of fuck
but it was still a swear
and my grandfather
liked to call people
pips, an insult.
i guess this is regional
but integrity,
labia,
i mean, you've heard those words before,
right?

## MY PAIN

i feel lonely a lot
i really do
supposedly there's
something wrong with that
but how could it ever be
any other way,
all by myself
inside this body.
fleshy houses that
no one ever visits
though sometimes they knock,
ring the bell and run.

that weird shape on the floor
is my brand new boots
shiny & black as trash bags.
i was going to wear them
but i like my body better
in jeans right now, the flash
of my belt, tough.
earlier i wanted the fattest skirt
to crash across my thighs
i can't stay still
that's my problem
all the flat eyes
wanting a map of the void
you think they'd know better,
alone like that inside themselves

## THE CRUELTY OF STRANGERS

a guy made fun of my heart today
he called it an apple.
i don't understand this
human compulsion towards
cruelty
would i ever make fun
of a tattoo i didn't know,
waiting for food
in the bagel shop? no.
i am never mean to
strangers. i save it
for people i know,
the deserving.
you i would not hit
or punch or smack
but i would like to watch
someone else do it
not a stranger but a girl,
someone like me someone
who really deserves
to kick you in the stomach.
someone with really good boots.
connecting with the soft rolls
of your belly. *oomph.*
ever get the wind knocked
from your lungs? it's scary.
i would like to see you
on the sidewalk like that,
a fish out of water
but i won't do it.

if you were brave enough
to stand in my face
with your stupid advice
i would gently remind you
that we are not friends.
you live at the very bottom
of the sea

a dark and cloudy place
with absolutely no light,
just big sluggish ocean things,
probably slimy,
that sit forever in the sand,
no day and no night
so why do you think
you are qualified
to discuss this girl who is actually a lion
or a mountain,
something big out of nature
something with excellent
presence.
i'm not a dummy you know
i can, like,
pick my friends
and nothing's going
to work me over
like you and your salty
barnacled hands
miss pearly lip soft eye
the face that once looked
angelic
now strikes me as
mildly retarded.
goodbye.
back to the girl
with the excellent presence.

i'm trying to appreciate nature
but all i get are
peach lilies
in a vase
at the bagel store.
can i write a powerful essay
on the transcendental nature
of nature
leaning on the glass counter

waiting for my onion with
dill cucumber to arrive
and those things
on the sidewalk,
you call that a tree?

## UNSMOKING

grizzled,
what does that word mean?
i think that i am grizzled today,
walking down the sidewalk
in boots packed with sand
from last week's beach

the fire was almost dead,
bricks of wood like a little city
that's just been bombed
and then the man
walked out of nowhere
and threw his shirt on the pyre
just like that, big snarly guy
eco-warrior, i kept calling him
thor.

but back to grizzled
and me on the street
thinking about chemical peels
like sandblasting your face
i think i would like one.
like a scar or tattoo,
a wrinkle portrays
a certain experience.
the experience of dehydration,
revealed.
do i really do it so much more,
drink, smoke
this body like a car,
pedal to floor
am i using up heartbeats
reserved for 70, 75
what will happen.

tracy wrote her phone number
on this matchbook
i light my cigarette with

switching to camels
choosing cancer over
emphysema, aunt ella
walking to the corner and
turning back, breathless.
she can't stop smoking either,
even with her rich daughter
bribing her with trips to atlantic city.
she stops for a month,
goes gambling
lights back up.
i will quit now, my new
pack fresh on my windowsill
where i am always smoking
i need a room with windows
to connect me to the world,
keep me out there even
when i have to be in
i'm about ready
for my period to be over
i am refusing to comply
with my menstrual cycle,
putting away my tampons
the stubborn drip in the crotch
of my jeans, staining
my thighs
and i'm supposed to dance
naked tonight, with
my bloated belly and dangling
string, bah.
what is wrong with today.
no one has energy,
where did the energy go
even the cars beneath my window
move slow and the children
look confused.
i get phone calls,
laurie, sini,
patricia needs a beer
i quit, i say, for my

bloated face. patricia's
grizzled too today
and summer is getting into
an RV and leaving.
she's got that girlfriend
the one that stopped her
from leaning into my lips
that time, also in a window,
right at the treetops.
*you're just drunk* she said
yeah i am but i like you
i burped and kissed her
mildly resistant lips
which were red and sexy
she looked like john travolta
but young, and a girl
goodbye to summer and her
girlfriend traveling the lanes
of our country.
i sit, solid
in my windowsill,
unsmoking.

## BITER

i lost the poem
i woke up with.
it was dangerous
something beautiful
about victory
and danger
i woke up with it
spilling into the white
of your room the fat brown towers
of boxes
packed tight
with your whole
life.

the beautiful poem
slipped away
and there you were
sleeping
your magnificent
sleep.

inside the night
i bit you.
why
am i compelled
to act like such a shit
around you, i mean,
i like you
a lot.
you kick my ass
with your eyes,
every glance,
*wham*
i'm struck
yet i can't
stop
chewing your arm
like the excitable puppy

i become
in your presence.

i must confess
i live
for this exquisite
nervousness
rushing like coffee
through all my body's
tunnels.
the luxury
of your hands
at my throat
before sleep.

lucky me,
i get to fall
to sleep
beside
the sun. there she is,
sleeping darkly
like the cat
on the chair,
commanding
unconsciousness
like she commands
attention
in the light.

this girl
is a meal
am i making
that clear
a crescendo
of sleep
keeping me awake
and biting.

## PLEASE

call me call me call me
on the phone
where the computer glows
all night long
a church
for the weirdo electrical
entities
people psychic
or drugged
can detect
whispering
in their crackly voices
more technology
just call me.
i'm playing that
motley crue album
the one you have
with vince neil's
enormous
leather
crotch
on the cover
his warbling voice
high enough
to call him sissy.
so
why aren't
you calling me
when i called you
and left a message
that i really want
to see you
are you on a date
with that perfect
looking girl
that i saw you with
when my hair looked so
shabby

and you lifted me
into the air
by my crotch
just fucking call me
i'm sitting here
plucking a flea
from my leg
dropping it out the window
imagining it using
air itself
as a springboard
to push its nasty legs on
and hop right back in
these are 3rd
generation fleas,
invincible.
they just
keep coming
and you
don't call.

## MOTORCYCLE FUNERAL ESCORT

he said, I'm Sorry, and,
I'm Not Gonna Interrupt You
as he crouched at our thighs
and interrupted.
he's a writer too he
saw us writing he's
a taxi driver he's
gonna move to new york city
because it's just too easy here,
no stories, too easy, people
just give you money, people
are so nice with their manic-
depression and do we like
cabbies? he had lots of things
he could give us, lots of ideas
and if we don't like cabbies
he got bikes do we like bikes?
he said, I Really Understand
Your Femininity, he said it to Sini
in her goggles, greasy hair smooshed
beneath her snaggle hat, big loop
of steel swinging
from her nose.
he said, I Understand and I thought
what that we're dykes
that the first thought to hit
our feminine heads
when a guy like that kneels
at our feet
at a bar
is how fucked up is he
would he be easy to roll
how much money he got there
would it be worth it
this guy's got big holes in his shirt
but still the thought is there.
he wants to take us to the next level
You Know, The Next Level,

I Can Take You There, The Next
Level, level what level Sini
asks the top of the bar what
level what the fuck
are you talking about?
the next level, he's frustrated
obviously we don't get it
it could be beautiful
he could tell us some stories
look, i say, we're writing
our own, it just breaks
a man's heart, watching
a girl so involved with her life,
without him like that.
he gave us his card.
Gary Sartor, taxi service
to airports. I Don't Do
Motorcycle Funeral Escorts
Anymore, he said. great.
thanks. Yeah Thanks, he says
leaving.
Have A Nice Life.
he sat back down
at the end of the bar.

## NO GIRLS
for sini

sitting at the bar
where are the girls

home dialing and hanging up
        dialing and hanging up

walking the street
poking a head
into all the wrong holes
looking for something
she doesn't want,
not really.

dialing and hanging up
dialing and hanging up

this is not a bar
for girls and we are not
girls inside this bar.
something more eternal,
something better
than that.

a strange configuration
in the sky happening only once
in many civilizations.

girls are everywhere
on this planet
how many girls are there
millions
too many and there are only two of us.

i thank god for her
she thanks god for me too

## DIVE

time spent talking to you is time spent
between the roof and the ground at the bottom,
the slow fall through cups of coffee, shredded meat
i didn't even know i was airborne until
my body met with sick sour pavement
and you walked up the sidewalk, gone.

for you i would fold up my entire life like a
playskool pretend city, packing in all
the cafes, glass bus stops, the dealers on the corner
always thinking i need something they got.

when people write those poems about this place
where i live, kicking needles down the street and
o the whores and o the cracked junkies with faces
like a busted couch and o the trash the filth the
swirl of spray paint on the wall, well,
it always makes me wonder where they lived
before.

i say this because i feel you down here with me,
this thing i have for you, it is as noble
as being wronged from birth, is as fierce
as a fight for something impossible
that i know you understand.
wait. i will. it is like sleeping,
how it keeps you still
and fills your head with pictures.

## ASK ME ABOUT MY GRANDKIDS

i pick a charles bukowski book from the couch
grab my ice tea and walk down the hall.
when i'm done with the book i'll buy another
and another, he wrote so many i can do this
forever, he's dead and more shit keeps coming,
he won't go away. what is it about charles.
i think i finally love him, i imagine his room
dim and yellow, packed with pages, shit everywhere,
blowing around the place if hollywood had breezes.
breezes blow everything around my room
i throw half of my weekend away
and the rest goes into a suitcase for later,
to show to my grandkids:
this is when i got a sunburn in la
driving in a car that did not accurately represent
my tax bracket, beside a  girl who loved to drive it
handing her cigarettes the whole time, she took them
with skinny fingers, grey-tipped and i kept noticing her hands
all weekend, they were cool taking the cigarettes from my hand
and i'll probably never look at her fingers so much again
now that i'm in love and have destroyed everything.
i'll tape her in my scrapbook next to all the girls
she doesn't want to be around. this one was
going to ride the country with me, this one kept rats,
let them run through her bed, this one was a brilliant
writer, she could have been my protégé or something
i tell it to my grandkids. i eat chef boy-ar-dee ravioli
and the meat sticks in my teeth. the corner store
was the farthest i could walk today and the selection
is bad. a big bottle of ice tea. something to keep me
alive. is this my muse? this is pathetic.
love is frightening and most things run
from its shadow. it must be like your favorite tv star
turning on the screen and saying You, I See You.
extending a real arm from the glass.
you think you'd love it but it's terrifying.
when i finally did meet big bird i ran screaming.
i was five years old in a department store

and the nightmares kept me twitching all night.
set me back into the magazine,
into the pages of your own flat scrapbook.

## OH GOD

spilling water from my back,
you call and i come.
that exhausted walk to reach you
breathless and no i didn't run
to see you, i've been smoking
too much, same thing.

another awkward hug in the car
as my face smashes your cheek
that i can feel it leaving now
is the saddest, a beautiful eruption
you could have picked it off the tree
and chowed

but you weren't hungry.
feeling it dying away all day
much worse than the straining
against the leash, another gorgeous
thing that should not have happened,
gone again.

## IF YOU LEAVE A WOMAN FLOWERS
## YOU'LL PROBABLY SCARE HER AWAY

i dreamt my pubic hair curled long
down my leg i dreamt
she was so close i could see
the cracks in her lips and
people kept walking in i dreamt
of reading poetry in some hick
country town i dreamt we were
together in this bed that was a cloud,
i turned like a sunflower to her lips
and found a middle-aged stranger,
like the sun went out.
dreams
are like that and life
is like that ten second limbo
between waking up and memory
sounding a dog whistle
to the disappointment
that sinks your chest like a wrecked
souffle.
i just think it sucks
that she did it at a party,
he said, it's really mean
to break your heart at a party.
she could've done it on the phone
or at least in a place where there
was no one else around,
so i wouldn't have to slip
into the bathroom one step ahead
of crying, sit on the toilet
with my eyes swelling red and worry
about all the whiskey i drank
to impress her, how it is climbing slowly
up my throat like kudzu
and my best friend is shoving
little pieces of paper under the door
with her name on it like a bad dream,
he doesn't know I've just been dumped

even though i wasn't dumped really,
you need a relationship to be dumped you
need a foundation to be dumped off from and
all i had was three long kisses that
spit out hope and poetry like
a catholic woman spitting out babies,
blind to birth control and reality
three long kisses that turned on themselves like
cancer cells, making me need her face
above a cup of coffee telling me
the story of her life and
she says these interactions
are interfering
with getting to know me better,
she says,
the irony.
and all these heartless boys
slumped drunk in a half-empty room
saying you should've just kissed her,
you really blew it, you
should've just fucked her and forgot her—
don't they have souls?
how did they get so lucky
to lose their hearts for good when
mine keeps finding its way back
with a nose like a dog
only to get sucked from my throat
again and again
she's a heartbreaker, this poet warned me
and this poet should know,
she's got a chest full of cracks
from the girls she let skate across
her heart's thin ice,
i should've listened.
and let me tell you how
there is a full color portrait
of this heartbreaker
chalked in front of her house
by an admiring friend.
she lives on my street.

the world is so small in san francisco;
it is closing in on me
like a necktie.
i step on her face
on my way to the store.

## 1/1/94

i knocked on her door
3:00 in the morning new year's day
i was drinking whiskey at the heterosexual
grunge party in the apartment right
next door to her own thought the
slur in my voice would maybe be a
turn on you know how these san
francisco dykes like their women
out of control and dangerous so i
leaned in the hallway banged
my knuckles on the glass of her door and
she answered
happy new years i was in your building
just thought i'd come by and say
happy new years i wondered
if my alcoholic stench had
hit her yet and if she was impressed
and i can't remember if she told me that she was
stoned or if it was the way her eyes
were wetly pink beneath her glasses she
was busy watching a tv movie robert duvall
treating his family like shit sounds great
i said thinking fuck she knows i wrote an
obsessive love poem about her and now she
thinks i'm a freak, well, don't let me keep you
from that robert duvall movie i said and
she said yeah i better go
happy new year.

## LETTER TO A MASOCHIST

that posturing narcissus who
walked abreast
the envied assaults of me
(observing, cry by cry,
book and book, to be victim, perpetually)
has nothing on you,
o my love,
o my scarred criminal, who
with one tit
clamped (you might say) in the mind-fuck
of cock and past
slithers with the other down deep
in magnificent cathedrals of the trusted
flesh-workers,
transfixed by the deliberate wound.

## SUICIDE POEM

all of my friends have such complete control
over their lives. they can kill themselves
any time they want to. right now
laurie can jump out my open window
or she can get up and go to the bathroom.
erich can swallow cleanser. peter
can hang himself. another can take her
new gun and tilt it into her mouth's
wet hollow. the many with their sharp
things can just keep going. they could
tear a vein and they'd know exactly
what they were doing, having taught
themselves the body sure as any surgeon.
if they want it they can have it.
they know it and they keep themselves
alive, all by themselves.
it seems so huge. it seems impossible.
it seems like more of them would be gone.
all things considered i think i will
just stay quiet and let them wear
their dysfunctions like feather boas.

## WHEN I LOVE MY FATHER

not at the thought of his childhood,
leather belts in the air like wires
a storm knocked down and the things
he learned to do, to take pieces of
his self and i don't know if he
killed them maybe he just put them
away, shoved them into the wet of
his intestines, inside and hiding.
he learned to drink, also, and when
he learned to stop, pride shiny
as a boy, how my mother became
his parent then, passing shame like
heirlooms she kept his victories quiet.
but really these things touch me as much
as print in a psychology textbook, they
are grooves worn in the vinyl of my mind,
a thousand talkshows yakking.
when that feeling comes and comes quick
it is a lightswitch thrown in my chest,
bright as lightning it sends cockroach
anger scuttling toward the cracks in my
ribs. when it comes it comes with thoughts
of food he ate, yoo hoo and fried spam,
things tasting of sweet fake raspberry,
warm weather lime rickeys in big plastic
cups rocking with ice and green domes
of fruit, a shot of za-rex and fizz.
we would make them for each other,
leaving tabletop sticky
with pulp and syrup.
and just because it ought to,
the poems he wrote in a hand
that looked female do not
move me. it is the boxes of cookies
he'd hide beneath his chair the way
an older brother would it is the young thing
inside him that pulled down his face like
the brick of a building crumbling in

an earthquake and all because i ate the brownie
he'd been dreaming about eating, a reward
for hours spent lifting the death-stuffed
bodies of the old, his nurse pants spotted
with the red and brown colors of sickness.
that chocolate tasted guilty in my mouth,
he felt like my son and who was he, exactly
and who is he now and what is this little-girl
fear of his death or my death and sadness big
and red and absurd as the Kool-Aid man crashing
through my head with pitchers of compassion well
i'm not thirsty, i've heard his wife plead his case
ruthless as any lawyer, holding up books
and jewelry as proofs of his love as if love
was the point, love like a ticket buying you
unlimited access to another and i've heard my old
lover phoning him with violent threats,
his eyes rolling on her palm like that santeria saint,
proofs of his evil as if evil was the point,
as if he was anything other than a man,
sad and sick and impossibly common.
my arms are bent and rusted as scales
from the absolute weight of their black
and their white. somewhere in the center,
my father and i, tied like damsels
to our own separate tracks.

## NANABELLY

my grandmother lies
in a coma
at the bottom of my belly.
she comes to sometimes,
in the back of a cab driven
by a man taking the long way home
because he thinks i'm young and stupid,
she stirs with each flick
of the digital meter. paint fumes, too,
they bring her up like smelling salts,
the smooth movement of the brush,
push of paint onto wall,
her yoga.
and cigarettes, she never
let the smoke reach her lungs
but it sickened them anyway,
butts greasy with lipstick,
whole ashtrays of them like
dining room centerpieces.
she thought psychics were charlatans but
she went to them anyway, one told her
she'd live till a hundred.
she died at fifty
to the purgatory of my stomach,
waking now and then
to remind me not to sit on toilets.

## ADVICE FOR THE LOVELORN

i remember ali told me
you can't stalk someone you know,
they'll just turn around and
talk to you, make your tongue swell
with dumbness make
your brain go into hiding.
linda said oh
i'm not into the crash and burn,
i'd rather get amnesia for the first three months,
come out of it when we've learned to communicate.
i remember judith told me
you're like a lesbian woody allen and
heather-in-the-know said
go slow, like i've got a crush
on some skittish animal and my
intensity is a cage.
this woman,
she had a poem once
and the words
nailed my heart
to the idea of her.
i remember matt told me
it is the noblest pursuit,
what else is there to live for?
we were sitting by the Charles at sunset with
a sixty-dollar bottle of
champagne too warm to drink and
oil-slick ducks sailing through the
trash, yeah, romance and activism
and the art that bursts
from heartbreak and anger,
i'm thinking maybe,
if i learned to throw those sex vibes,
got a heroin habit,
something romantic,
start drinking too much and
smashing glass in bars.
i remember tabrina told me,

we were talking about that woman
who seems to never be in love,
she said
maybe she's one of them healthy people,
she's got her career,
art,
those workshops in the mountains.
some people
don't need obsessive love affairs to get by
some people
do not feel compelled
to push their heart onto a stick
and roast it over someone's fire.
well those people suck, i said.
what kind of passionless monsters
live their lives like that?
that pull
in your belly
is grace,
remember when i tell you.

## TRYING TO MOVE THE MYSTERY MUSCLE
for robin

is wanting to piss into
a urinal penis envy?

she bucks her hips knees
straight and piss bounces
off porcelain like my sister,
a sick little baby power puking
Similac across the living room,
its as strong as a SuperSoaker
any woman can do it,
she says,
just drop that female muscle,
*let it go* but
i can wiggle both my ears,
i know that some muscles are secret,
you just can't find them but
lots of women do this,
*sure,*
*projectile pissing,* says the dyke behind the bar
pushing glasses of water and ice my way
and the tough girl in the cowboy hat,
she can rotate her hips hula-hoop style
tossing urine in great golden rings.
in the bathroom, blue light bouncing
disco off the urinals i am drunk
from abandoned pints of backwash
Anchor Steam, dumping them straight
back throat to bladder
*stop laughing,* she coaches,
*just drop that muscle and go*  and
i remember her impossible firehose spray,
it looked like fun i
tilt my hips and the drunk girls
behind me all giggle i push,
reach deep for that mystery muscle
and piss all over myself
dribbling down over leggings, boots,

the bathroom floor sludgy as
a new york curb in winter
*awwwwwww, you can do it* she
says with a swing of her hips and
one more bullet of piss
girl, if i can do it
*and woman can* and
she's so sincere,
big eyes begging confidence
she tells me
i'll ejaculate when i cum
if i master
that thick red muscle
(she does)
and i practice,
squirting into my shower,
straddling my toilet backwards till
the seat is as messy as a boy
but that muscle
is elusive as uterus,
i just can't
find it.

## HOW TO REPROGRAM YOUR SEXUALITY

realize that you never had a chance.
you were born into this place
where they pump pornography in like oxygen,
i don't mean hustler and all that shit, either,
i mean marlboro and l'oreal and the brady bunch.
you work your way up to hustler,
you've got to start somewhere.
maybe you should take
a college-level psychology course or something.
mine taught me that stressed out moms
make gay babies and schizophrenic geniuses
drawing maps of the universe should be locked up
but also how you can flash things like shoes
on a screen with a naked lady and after not too long
the men in the audience will get a hard-on
from a single spiked heel.
it should make you a little angry
to find yourself so programmed, but don't go
beating up women. do what i do.
walk into liquor stores and shred the
st. paulie girl ads in the proprietor's face,
have a little argument about how you're
a fanatic and why aren't you working
to make sure all those corporate women
are making as much as all those
corporate men, something important,
he'll say, but that's ok,
maybe what is important is having a sex fantasy
that doesn't come from a box, one that madonna
wouldn't bother making into a video, where
the woman looks like a woman and not a barbie doll,
i mean, you're a grown man, doesn't it
embarrass you to be lusting after
barbie dolls? maybe you've never thought of it
that way, maybe you've never thought of it at all,
how everything that turns you on is
also everything that turns everybody else on
which is also everything that everyone

from budweiser to the gap
is hoping you'll be turned on by
so that you'll push some of that sexy green stuff
their way and maybe you want to think about this
and decide that your sexuality
should be more than the sum
of some not-so-subliminal advertising,
your father's pornography and whatever
relative molested you during childhood
but far be it from me to pull you from
your lipstick fishnet fuck paradise,
you're a grown man,
you can make up
your own mind.

## ALL THESE WOUNDED WOMEN
(hear me, jessica)

it was like i should be a little nervous,
falling in love with all these wounded women
the way my sister in high school kept falling in love
with assholes,
as if there was anything else to choose from and
show me a woman who is not a walking
open wound and i could maybe
take the challenge
of finding what she's hiding,
here is jessica, the most well-adjusted
girl in the world she let me claw her palm
when i got my tattoo she was flipping through
a Skin Art saying things like Chain Yourselves Together
By Your Bellybutton, That's Not Co-Dependent,
clucking her tongue at the woman who kept corseting
till she died at eighty,
bottom ribs crushed as eggshell.
i said Wasn't There Ever Anything,
An Eating Disorder, Drugs, and she tells me
about a single bad relationship,
four years ago. she worries about me,
smoking cigarettes drinking coffee
getting crushes on girls who make themselves
bleed
i said I See Where You're At,
I Don't Think It Counts
Unless You Had To Fight To Get There,
Any Self-Mutilations Or Suicide Attempts,
Did The Sponge
Of Your Psyche Ever Soak Up A Lie
That Worried Your Cunt And Your Dreams,
How Exactly Did You Happen?
in the tattoo parlor jessica has
the boy who does the piercings
give her a surgical steel tour of
drawers of clamps and needles kept her
talking all week about girls tearing holes

in their skin. those conversations
pulled defense from my body like venom,
tucson air too hot for arguing leaving me slumped
in her home like a wilting houseplant.
seven safe nights i slept in her bed,
dreaming of dangerous women and
waking to walls of mountain curved
as breast and hip. again in san
francisco choking on smoke and
pabst blue ribbon i flash my new
tattoo and let my fingers trace light
on the arm of another, skin raised
and dark she asks how good
did it feel like the woman who told me
the swirl on her spine was like
getting fucked hard and i say i
tried i tried to reach that transcendental
endorphine blast, tried to make it
feel like sex but it remained
what it was, pain like a patch of grass
on fire and spreading hear me, jessica,
the body makes some choices on its own it
does not ask your opinion.
it slams the door of nerve and cell
in the face of your brain,
that know-it-all.

# FOR ZANNE FOR ZANNE FOR ZANNE

o my darling your eyes are strange soft
ocean things that big-bellied humans
would dig up and eat raw they are
puddles and slugs and i know when
i've stepped on them by the way they squirm.
o my darling your hair melts into my sink
like childhood, yours, and you choose your
age by the hats you wear. you are everything
kindergarten i press my hands to your face
like elmers glue and peel you off my palms.
o my darling your mouth is a tenement
packed with immigrant relations and there's
always more on the way it smells like food and
cigarettes and i want to live there too.
o my darling you are all science-fiction,
you are a dog from another planet and
the fear you smell's your own.
o my darling your armpits are mouths you
can't quiet doors you can't lock,
i breathe in words like dinner.
o my darling your feet are so human,
they think gravity's a bad parent that
lied about santa and god they press
against your shoes like barnacles.
o my darling you are geography and
history you have mapped a life across
your skin and let me hike there.
o my darling, you smart-girl, you
lava-brain you are blue blue blue you're
blood's honest color you have word games
in your gut, crossword puzzles, scrabble
and a thick thick thesaurus heart.
o my darling you are that crazy toy
from my playpen all dizzy spinning plastic
honks the jack in the box keeps scaring me
and some doors just won't open.
o my darling you sleep like a fleshy dream
like i could just walk into your ears o

my darling you are my favorite pen that
keeps losing ink and coming back and
chopping through all my poetry o my
darling your kneecaps are oracles i
touch your legs like language i am
conjugating your hips your shoulders and
your belly your belly your belly.

## WE COULD BE SOULMATES

hey now tall girl
aren't you bored
all by yourself in your messy room
smoking pot till your head spins
out of your pillow
don't you want to be my
sister we can cut
ourselves open and
share what's inside smear it
altogether so there's a forever
with my name sliding through
your veins we could be
bloodsisters like two sweaty girls
in a backyard hideout you know
it might sound catholic or
it might sound cliche but you
look like the virgin to me and
i want to be that holy child
chewing at your nipple
i've seen you
moving down valencia your
sharp bones poking at your clothes
when you walk it looks like dancin' and
hey there tall girl
don't you know you
sucked the heart right
out of my throat
this is serious
we could be soulmates you
are in my dreams like destiny
got me tossing back shots of whiskey shots
of scotch trying
to get back
to the taste
of your
teeth
i'm waxing alcoholic, trying
to get back to the smell

of your mouth
breathe it into my face
like a kind of masturbation
tall girl don't you know
not to be givin' tattoos with
your eyes and when you
curl those lips like
the most perfect wave i
wish i was a surfer,
i'm not even blonde i
found a recipe for desperate seduction
in the back of this book you need
cinnamon ground antler and the
pulverized eggshell of an
infertile dove but
it's enough to call out prayers
for the accident of seeing you
on the street your tall head poking
the sky hey there
tall girl
don't you want a sister or
at least a cup of
coffee?

## THREE MALE ABORTION DOCTORS
for bruno g

you know, the three abortion doctors
shot were men, ok? they were men.
maybe you should just think about that.
i had just ended a poem
about the way little boys
                              hit
                                  little girls,
when i feel these thick fingers poking
at my shoulder blade and the angry
man behind me starts yelling about
                              male
                                  abortion
                                      doctors.
i am having a hard time understanding
the point he is trying to make: is it
that men are sacrificing themselves
in droves
for the noble cause of
women's reproductive
rights?
is he saying that men
are the real victims
of this abortion war
or is he just a man
whose guilt clangs
like a church bell
when he hears the truth
of a woman's experience?
*think about it*, he yells it with meaning,
like the words could rock my world,
could change my life and i like
challenges, i can't say no to a dare,
i think about the men
who are dead now
because their lives were spent scraping
those tumorlike pieces of flesh
from the insides of women's bodies and

if you want to know the truth,
i am a bit suspicious of doctors,
and the half-knowledge they tug around like gold
and i am a bit suspicious of male doctors
who, my mother told me, see hundreds
of naked bodies all the time and it's just a body,
they don't think anything of it and sorry,
i never bought it, like doctors
are immune to misogyny like doctors
don't buy pornography and rent whores
like doctors were spared the upbringing
that works a woman into something to fuck
own and control and i am thinking
about three male abortion doctors
and i am thinking about control,
like the control of a man's hand aiming a pistol,
the control of a man's hand entering a woman's body,
the control men have over women's lives, because
if you ask me to look at this scene
a man with a lot of personal control
over women's bodies
was killed
by a man who wants more personal control
over women's bodies, well,
i just see men,
stretched out in lines like highways
their hands filled with guns,
with speculums, with paychecks
penises, power, control and where
are the women
who lie with legs spread, waiting
for the man to undo the damage done
by the last man the legs were spread for
and her fight inside,
hacking at people
like they were heavy jungle weeds
blocking her trail and the women
who help her cut through,
sharp women with dagger tongues
and scythes for hands and

there are women in this picture,
somewhere,
women doctors and women patients,
women who find the whiteness
of hospital walls and men
too alienating, women
who find the prices and laws
too impossible
and those women don't need
a man's gun
to end this abortion debate
they've got coathangers,
closets full,
and i'm sorry
that this is all your challenge inspired,
just more anger from one of those tired,
angry women always bitching about men
and the way they rape, the way they control,
the way they project infinite scenarios
with a single *hey baby*
i'm sorry bruno g,
but this is all i could do.

## DRAGGING THE RECYCLING
## OUT OF THE WHOREHOUSE

dragging the recycling out of the
whorehouse because i am a
big strong lesbian whore with
boots on my feet. this girl
let me borrow them but my foot
pressed into the sole and made
them their own so she had to let
me keep them and i tried
to make a similar imprint
on the girl a kind of spiritual
footprint but i failed and now
i've got these boots that i wear to
drag the recycling out of the whorehouse
thinking i must look like such a freak the
green marin landscape behind me the wind
blowing my wig into lipstick this
flashy danceclub dress and hose slipping
down my leg like catholic school knee
socks and i am such an unhealthy
prostitute sitting around drinking mountain
dew and smoking all the other whore's
cigarettes i burnt my wig lighting them
on the gas stove i wish i could bring
my friends to work we could read tarot
cards and write and chat on the
sunny country patio of the quaint
northern california whorehouse and
i would say excuse me and totter off
to the bedroom to tend to men who
think it's their privilege to rent
women because they are all such
big king jesus superheroes. do
i sound bitter about my job?
i am but
no more than ever so i
dragged the recycling out of the
whorehouse like last night dragging

it out of my own house and my
roommate laurie didn't even help and
i love her for that why should she it's
my fucking chore so i did it myself in
my feety pajamas leaving armfuls of
bottles like cookies for all the
homeless santas the shopping carts
patrolled the block all night keeping
me awake that and every car door's
slam i thought it was a taxi delivering
that girl to my doorstep because i
couldn't believe she'd just blow
me off and not call back like she was
supposed to even if she was drunk and
at a party and watching sid and nancy,
that's a stupid movie. it's not even true.
nancy's mom tried to stop it and
so did johnny rotten. so i was awake
all night and if she had taken a taxi
to my house or maybe spent the day
calling every escort ad in the weekly
till she found me she would've made my
heart swell all big with manic love,
being such a sucker for dysfunctional
romance there are books for girls
like me women who love too much being
the obvious but don't forget smart
woman foolish choices and when helping
you is hurting me sometimes i think
the only difference between me and
my mother is time and place and choice
of hairstyle.

## BEACH POEM
for marya

on the beach sand dug at my knees
when the horses went by.
we held those dogs by chain and leather
collars of canvas biting my fingers,
patting their asses thick with salt and mud and
whispers to sit and not to chase
those big and dainty animals.
they passed us like prom queens
their tracks in the sand heel prints
on a gymnasium floor.
those dogs wanted to move so terribly their tongues
and tails could not be stilled. like the bad kids
in an urban schoolyard we kept them from
beating up the rich girls, the nerds, the teachers'
pets. sixteen gritty paws scratched at fur and sand,
strong necks pulled us into each other
before we let them fly to water.

## I AM THE LIGHT

here you are in my room again.
and i have all these brilliant feelings
too big to funnel into poetry.
art sucks too i mean the visual,
paint and thick color. what i
really want is to have sex
with you but i can't start that.
i'll beat you up instead, like
high school fags on the
wrestling team, kick your plaid
leg and a ballet move to
your butt. all that quiet
energy. i'm only playing.
you giggle and i want to
kiss you harder. i am sorting
through feelings like
a box of old clothes keep this throw
that out give that one away but
be sure you won't feel regret when
you see it looking good on
someone else. not smart to
feel too much in this
place where all the humans
are. cover it with blankets like
putting out a fire. last night at
a party was a dog that
looked like my mother, i
kept saying that dog over
there looks just like my
mother! and you
are like her with me
thinking say the right thing the
right move right amount of self-
sacrifice and cuteness and
she'll see the light. and
you are like her but here
i am the light.
and then your poem came into

my head like a stained glass
revelation, I Just Wish I
Would Occur To You, and
i didn't even know it was
yours, i thought someone else
wrote it! and then pouting ridiculous
thoughts like just because someone
broke your heart you shouldn't
turn around and break another.
like you could cure it retrograde
with a kiss. better start dumping
my valentines into the mailbox
then. i'm smarter than that.
i just wanted to tell you that
i know how you felt. i just
wanted to tell you that
i am the light.

## A BRIEF NIGHT OUT IN TUCSON

his voice was thick with israel
he said someone
was trying to kill us
so we killed them first,
like all our holidays and i said
here's to self-defense and drank
expensive beer bought by
the straight boy who slides to
the edge of his seat
each time the woman beside me bites
my neck.
i said i don't put on shows
for straight boys so she
called me hostile,
that straight boy's her friend.
later i am smoking her cigarettes
picking flecks of tobacco from
my teeth and crunching on glass
from the guiness we broke open
on the curb i tell you bad sex
tastes like high school like
drinking too much it stinks
like cigarettes
in the front seat of her sports car
this other woman's face rose like a moon
behind my eyes until i opened the door
and spilled into the street.
you have a real problem with men she told me,
did you have a bad experience and i said
yeah my whole entire life's a
bad experience with men, that's why
i'm queer cause my dad was mean and
boys teased in kindergarten so it
scarred my sexuality but really i
subconsciously want one to rape me,
that's why i like tough girls with
dildos and maybe one day i'll meet
that Nice Boy that quintessential

soulmate who will give me
A Good Experience and i'll be cured so
why do you think you're gay?
one night out in tucson and already
my veins are screaming for san
francisco toxins a dysfunction junkie
trying to satisfy my fix with casual sex
in a camaro. i left my necklace broken
between car seats to make her sad
when she finds it, i left that town
on a greyhound it will be a long way
back.

## ODE TO CHELSEA

in chelsea there were always vans full of clowns
kidnapping children and mickey mouse tattoos
laced with lsd, there was always some
public school girl trying to kick my catholic school ass,
always some strange man needing to show me his penis
and spanish boys blowing kisses at me while
white boys called me slut, oh, chelsea,
bustling beneath that great green bridge eternally
dripping pigeon shit, chelsea with that muddy creek
sailing shopping carts and plastic bags and an
occasional murdered woman and before i was born
it all burnt down but after i was born
they built a mall on the ashes and
i was caught shoplifting lipgloss
in the kmart but never caught smoking cigarettes
in the public bathrooms, smoking was fun in chelsea,
so many empty lots to practice french inhaling,
so many piles of trash to set on fire and i
was on my way to the bank for my mom
when the camera crew stopped me and asked
what i liked best about chelsea,
i was wearing a purple sweatshirt over my
catholic plaid skirt, i was wearing grease
in my white trash hair and i said
i like the library, so proud to have lucked into
chelsea's fifteen minutes, i like the library
with the old librarian who makes fun of my
little sister and the tables of public school boys
trying to lift up my skirt and books about
the bermuda triangle and the lochness monster
and chelsea had beauty pageants each year,
i got Mini Miss First Runner-Up
with a trophy and carnations and a million
jealous little girl eyes and chelsea had football
and cheerleaders and i never learned to cartwheel,
i had to tumblesault, getting dead leaves in my
feathered hair and i could only do a half-split,
they let any girl on that sorry squad and chelsea

had free lunches in the park all summer
for the latchkey kids of deadbeat dads,
baloney and cheese with a bruised peach,
milk, warm orange juice and a soggy
ice cream sandwich and the park teacher
Jay pulled out his switchblade when i
made fun of his favorite band J Geils,
i was such a little troublemaker,
and chelsea, chelsea, my favorite park was the cemetery
with the spraypainted gravestones and men sleeping
in the mausoleums, i broke my wrist there,
riding Mandy's bicycle, chelsea, chelsea,
it's not even a city anymore, the mayor stole
all the town's money and now it's being run
by Boston University like a Fisher-Price playland,
chelsea, chelsea, my home town.

## AND I STILL CAN'T DRIVE, REALLY

i am inside the car
in the emptiest part of the desert
where the cactus had been brought down
to make room for cows and i am sitting
in the seat she always sits in, the trembling
machine awkward under my palms and i am
performing a three-point turn for the very first time,
working my neck into this impossible angle,
skinny arms twisting the wheel till it stops
and i make the car go backwards, right into the only sign
for miles, short, yellow and sun-dull it is
wedged deep into the metal of the car and
i had been doing so well, driving careful and
now she is hopping out of the car and pulling
up the sign with two strong hands,
she yells drive! and i do but it's still in reverse,
it goes backwards and she doesn't even scream,
just contracts every muscle in her face and
lets it freeze there like a mother's curse and
blood is spilling in great streams, like miracles, and
back inside the car we can glimpse a spot
of bone beneath all that gushing and
i am the hysterical one, she is calm, calmly going on
about how she has no feeling in her hand, none at all,
and what if i have given her permanent nerve damage
and what if they have to amputate my finger,
she will leave me if that happens and that
strikes me as incredibly unfair, it was an accident,
but she asks how could she see my healthy hand
beside her own sad stump and not hate me?
two coyotes cross the road before us and as it happens,
she does not loose her finger, she is fine
but for a small scar and the only person
brave enough to teach me how to drive was matthew,
who i never wounded,
he stayed with me as i wound the car through desert curves
and pulled it onto the shoulder to pick wildflowers. he taught me
to park in the lot of a tucson tourist trap where the people

were dressed too loudly to hit by accident and if i did
it wouldn't matter much anyway and i learned to drive a little,
enough to steer the car through all of indiana when we
left the west for boston, i even pulled it into gas stations
and rode it out again, i let the speedometer rise to 75
on the highway, passing trucks with a thrill and
how is it that once you learn to drive it's like you grow
as big as the car, you fill the space between your self and
the edge of the hood as it passes quick over pavement,
your feet have eyes as they play with the pedals
and it seems you could keep going forever.

## JUST WHAT THE WORLD NEEDS

i can say something cosmic like
our tongues opened naval chakras and
out marched a hundred and twenty-eight dakinis
licking lips bumping hips doing that shit dakinis do
and when you ran for the bus quick like that you
left some in my belly they need to see you they want
to go home
and i'd like mine back too.
i can say something dysfunctional like
it's me falling back on my past like a plate glass
window i'm gonna end up slipping on the shards
getting cut
bleeding
or how about i'm an animal just an animal
a dumb fucking animal with a nose that sniffs
and a tongue that licks and you are too
don't call don't call just
die pretty like marilyn monroe
leave me writing poems about closure and completion
stuffed with longing like a xmas stocking,
trivial gifts i don't need at all but better
than what i'll be writing weeks from now if
i find you on my doorstep shit like *never trust a man,*
*all men are dogs* and *men who needs them* cliche shit
i already knew anyway listen you left my stomach
spinning like a psychedelic drug toy you left my cunt
like a flower that won't stop unfolding left my friends
confused and a little upset left me kicking identity into
the gutter like a tin can every time i walk by your house
got me writing a fucking love poem like
girl meets boy just what the world needs one more
girl-boy love poem got me chewing on my tongue
like a secret i gotta tell again and again and
i've got your fingernails tucked under my sleeve,
lying sharp on my wrist, did you know you forgot them,
do you want them back?

## ST. CANDACE OF THE INCEST DAUGHTERS

candace
you were the nearest thing to saint i'd ever seen
you left us feeling like we had won a war
i remember i was still in my whore dress with
the fringe at the hem and how carrie cried as i told
the story, her forehead on my knees and i rubbed
her shaking shoulders, candace, you made me
think of miracles rising in the heat when you nursed
your child in that tucson diner me sucking on an
iced tea and the sour taste stayed in my mouth
all day, candace, your belief like a telegram
from god saying sorry your own momma thinks
you ain't worth shit here's this woman now and you
tell her you tell her about fucking her husband
on her living room couch and she'll tell you that
the money he gave you was meant to buy easter baskets
and you tell her he wanted you to call him daddy and
she'll tell you about her stepfather and a mom like
your own and you tell her here's fifty dollars and she
says i'll take it i got 500 in the bank and i'm leaving
him taking the kids gonna go to school gonna be a
midwife cause i love giving birth and he treats me
bad, i'm not letting men treat me bad anymore,
i'm not letting men put me down anymore, candace,
you meant it, you said thank you like your heart was
breaking like you never heard the word miracle
and now your voice on paper saying i think i'm going
crazy, and i feel responsible, writing that letter
like a blueprint for the revolution
making you think that some problems
have answers that some wars can be won
we just weren't thinking
about the way fear makes a little girl's
mouth go tight the way governments decide
what makes a mother and those girls
never slid from your cunt so they stay
while you go with the one they say you own,
that boy at your tit, gonna raise this one
right you said and your last letter

was a catalog of proof that mattered less
than anything, little girls with infections
little girls who bleed before they're ripe
little girls in the books he wraps around his
dick and shares with his son little girls
sleeping in his bed one at a time one
at a time always one at a time

## HAPPY

i love this city
too many girls smile at me when i walk
down the street and there goes a jogger
wearing nothing but skimpy shorts 2 nipple rings
and a smile and what about the one
in the castro who only ever wears a g-string,
all that skin and never any bruises,
it's as if people just leave him alone,
let him live his life with his ass hanging out.
i love this city
everything you need you can buy on the sidewalk
in the mission, that is, until the cops started coming
by and handing out fines and if
these guys could afford to pay a fine they
probably wouldn't be trying to sell you a
set of cookware for seventy-five cents
but i guess that hasn't occurred to the cops,
or the mayor, who used to be a cop and
once a cop always a cop, or so they say
but i love this city
every single night of the week i can find a cafe
to drink cups of bad poetry in, and they don't
look at me weird when i ask for soy milk,
or if the oat cakes are vegan,
it's a pretty flaky place.
dangerous, too.
i'll probably leave soon
because i'm getting really tired
of watching my back
and listening to stories
about those who let their eyes wander
but right now it's sunny,
and i was just walking down market street
getting smiled at by girls and giving all my change away
to punk rock kids who need to take a bus somewhere
or drink some beer or eat a hamburger
i don't know, i'm just glad i could help out,
i'm just glad i'm 22 and far away from my parents,

i'm just glad i'm alive,
and i mean that
in the most dramatic and cliché way possible,
i just love this city.

.

# OPPRESS ME BEFORE I KILL AGAIN

borrowed time press
1993

i don't need anyone to hold me
i can hold my own
i've got highways for stretchmarks
see where i've grown
                    - ani difranco

# MY LIFE IN 11 PARTS

1.
it is the cat.
it must be.
the house is old,
the floorboards shift
and creak
with the slightest weight,
the weight of your black cat
standing in front of the door
when you are in the bathroom.
you can hear her presence
from your seat on the toilet.
you are fourteen years old,
you are sneaking one of
your father's Newports,
flicking ashes between your legs
into the toilet, reading the TV Guide
someone left in the bathroom.
you are getting into
or out of
the shower
or you are masturbating.
it is the cat.
it must be.

2.
he didn't want to be a step.
that's how it happened.
what is a step, he asked,
and he was his own answer,
his own step
would order his father
to beat him,
made him eat a pile of pig fat
so that even now, a grown man,
he can't eat pork chops.
to make it legal we saw a judge
do you love him, she asked, and like

a bad tv movie we nodded, tears
in our eyes. afterwards we ate donuts.
you have two birthdays now, i was told.
the other father, the first one,
defended his honor drunkenly
in the local Moose club.
my girls, he slurred, or so i heard.
there were rumors.
the last time i saw him
was at a 24-hour truck stop. drunk,
he didn't recognize me as he laughed
at my pink hair, made fun
of my friends' torn clothes.

3.
it is on oprah every day.
women are crying on geraldo,
yelling on donahue
and ted danson does it
to his tv daughter
on the monday-night movie.
on video, a whole series
of sinister stepfathers.
it's enough to make
any girl nervous, it's
enough to put ideas
in anyone's head.
but
he cooks chili for me,
big spicy pots and
gives me rides in his car,
his baby, he has an earring,
took me to see billy idol and
he once played drums
for billy squier
at a party.
he is on my wavelength,
he is like me,
my friend.

4.
it is not the cat.
it can't be the cat.
this comes from the thin mouth
of your twelve-year-old sister
she stuffs the keyhole with cotton
and right now you would like some
for your ears because you don't
like what she is saying to you.
you give her a string of words
to wear like a talisman,
*no,*
*never,*
*he would never,*
*he loves us,*
and finally,
*how could you think*
*such a thing?*
it works.
it keeps her away from you
for five more years and
the cat that sits
at the bathroom door sits
in front of your bedroom now, too,
you can hear the floorboards creak
under her four fat paws and
you will not stuff your keyhole
with cotton, ridiculous.
it is the cat.
it is the cat.

5.
it makes you feel better
to know you're not alone.
it is quite common,
having sexual fantasies
about your father, it
was the basis of Freud's
whole career, it's classic.
they aren't exactly fantasies,

but how else to categorize
this obsession you have
with your father watching
at your bedroom door.
this fear must be longing
twisted inside out, yes,
it is easier to bend
over backward than it is
to sit up straight
with your own eye
pressed
against that keyhole,
sometimes
you touch yourself
deliberately, lasciviously
you dance naked
around your room
bucking your skinny hips
collapse on your bed
with a cycle of thought:
if i really believed
he was out there
i could not have
just done that
therefore
he is not out there.
it becomes a ritual,
you make faces,
rub your cunt
like a good luck charm
and laugh at how strange
you are behaving.
this is how phobias
are born; neuroses
schizophrenia,
stick around.
you're a case study
in the making.
how unstable you are,
to turn obsessive-compulsive

by the presence
of your cat
at your door.

6.
you are nineteen and feeling guilty
for shutting your sister up.
the words *i thought so, too*
hang heavy in your chest, when
you let yourself think about it
they bang into your heart and
make your breath stop. all
you are acknowledging
is that you should not have
blown her off, you should not
have made her feel like a freak
for mistaking a cat
for a father. you only want
to apologize. and you find that
her suspicion has fermented
into a vinegary cynicism.
*i never stopped hearing the creaking*
she says. *i hear it still.*
and you remember your cat,
black with yellow eyes, how
she would slide out the front door
and return weeks later with tits
that wet your hands with milk
as you lifted her onto your lap.
and your head is spinning
with missing her and the frustration
of needing her sure form
curled on your belly
like a promise.
she ran away years ago.
*i never stopped hearing the creaking,*
you say.

7.
you have to pee.
you get up from the bed
you had just lied down in,
pull open your door and
there is your father,
standing in the dark.
he has one foot in the back hall
and two hands fumbling quickly
for the refrigerator door. *hungry,*
he says.  you tell this to your
new friend who is your sister,
and she tells you about sitting
on her bed and flicking
her middle finger
at her softly creaking door.
your house
seems to be shifting
into something different.
you had never noticed
the notches carved
into the bathroom frame.
when the door is shut
they form a small tunnel
connecting eyeball
to toilet-perched cunt.
the thought of your sister's
nimble fingers pushing
cotton into keyholes
makes you cry.  you check
your bedroom door for notches
and find nothing.  it is
your sister
who discovers the holes
in the back hallway.  she calls
you at your job and you don't
think those rubber legs of yours
are ever going to get you back
to that fishbowl of a bedroom
and the hallway

and the holes
patched lamely with tape
dry and linty
from being pulled back
all those times.
plug them up
with cotton, tape,
newspaper and
thick black nailpolish.
begin camping out
on your cold linoleum floor,
your head by the door.
you are setting a trap, a man trap,
you are trying to catch your father
doing something he
would never
do
and you are playing
with your sanity
like a slinky,
waking each morning
with an angry stomach,
old bones and a nose
stuffed with dust balls.
waking each morning
to your father
who smiles
as he hands you
the sandwich he made you
and drives you to work
in his car.

8.
there are explanations for everything.
two bored old men mashed british grass
into crop circles, uri geller
used friction to bend those keys and
any joe can hoax a ufo.
there are explanations for everything.
these days when you leave the bathroom

you meet your mother's new cat, waiting
expectantly at the door with pale blue eyes.
she is a kitten, too small to call
protesting creaks from the floorboards,
but she will grow.  you will never ask
your father if he used his artistry
and mathematical knowledge
to slice those fine holes in your wall.
only a yes would satisfy you,
all no's would be lies,
would never shut up
the accusing, paranoid
bitch who sleeps and wakes
in your head.
you do not want
the guilt made flesh
in the face of your father
it is your sister
who pulls the confession
from his cracked lips,
your strong scorpio sister
coaxing him with sweet bits
of sympathy and promises
of psychiatric help and
a vow to not tell mom.
and she means it,
at first.
she cries about keeping
the family together
as you hysterically stuff
everything you own
into a big nylon bag.
you want to free a scream
so loud
it leaves your throat bloody
you want it to streak the sky
like a chinese kite
as you run from the house
you live in.

9.
in light of the recent confession,
some incidents will begin to look
a little different.
the pile of Hustlers
in your father's drawer
that you looked through
when you were sixteen
remember
the punk-rock girls
how they looked like you
with fucked-up hair and ripped fishnets
and shaved cunts.
and how he'd whistle at you
when you left the bathroom
in a towel, *he was just*
*being cute,* she says, his wife.
and that time his friend maggie
wouldn't let him come over,
she's afraid i'll rape her, he said,
*maybe i would.* and his
preoccupation with the third reich
does not seem intellectual now,
how he had said
*if i was in germany*
*i would have been*
*a good little nazi*
and everyone laughed nervously,
including you. how
could you not have seen
what a dangerous man
he is, how was it
that you all just let him
into your house like that,
with no references or anything,
he was a stray male,
what exactly
were you expecting?

10.

mom says he's sorry and
jan who lives next door, whose
husband molested his niece
when he was eighteen, says
*don't say molestation, abuse,*
*rape, i had a man touch me,*
*paw me, put his tongue*
*in my mouth and you can't*
*compare that to a pair of cold eyes*
*eyes don't touch,* she says
and mom says
it wasn't physical
and he says
it wasn't sexual
he was just in awe
of his daughters
he would watch them reading
books in their beds.
and what about the hole
in the bathroom, well,
*don't say the word cunt,*
she says, *and what am i*
*supposed to do, then,*
*be a lesbian?*
her therapist says
the problem is codependency,
she should go to group
and why do your daughters
want to tell everyone
what happened? the grandfather,
it would kill that old man,
that tough old man
who went to war
at age sixteen and
still has dirt from
the trenches beneath
his nails. just
stay quiet.
my mother,

her lungs
and makeup
growing thicker
she is going to move to florida,
she is going to kill herself
and just cremate her,
she doesn't want a funeral
if everybody's fighting.

11.
move out.
move in with your girlfriend.
it will strengthen your relationship
because all you have in common
are the men who abused you.
read The Courage To Heal twice
but ignore the section
on prostitution
when your sister calls crying
at three o'clock in the morning
every morning
try to swallow all her pain
and end up sick.
write a ten page letter
to your father and
leave copies on the shelves
of the public library.
meet your mother in the city
for coffee.
cry.
take your bad relationship
on the road.
tucson.
back to boston.
stop talking to your mother.
just stop.
provincetown.
boston.
stop fucking men
for money.  go back

to tucson. your girlfriend
is nicer, but straight.
it ends
like an omen,
like an egg cracking.
crawl from it all
with muck on your skin
and watch things get better.

## MY MOTHER GETTING DIVORCED

she kicked that man
out of her house - well,
he kicked her out,
and her two kids, too, but
either way he is gone and
*first i was afraid*
*i was petrified*
*kept thinking i*
*could never live*
*without you by my side*
she is singing she is taking
over her children's stereo
madonna billy idol and wham!
slide to the floor, she is careless
she is fearless she is dancing
through the house to gloria gaynor
*oh no not i, i will survive*
and seeing this weak woman
rise up strong and kick across
the living room does not make
her children smile and cheer
it is just one more freaky
fucking thing, one more crazy
mood swing, and anyway,
right now it's
*go on now go*
*walk out the door*
but tonight she
will be crying with dionne
*why do you have to be a*
*heartbreaker*
*when i was being who*
*you want me to be*
and so her kids aren't buying it,
they crowd in front of mtv
and wait for the return
of their stereo
while their mother,

that wild woman,
takes that small chunk of freedom
the first time it's ever hit her hands
and she squeezes it, she works it
she knows how things leave quick,
chased away by the pounding
of an ex-husband at the door
or the promise of a new husband
in the sly glances of a strange man
she is a woman between men,
she is lightening, she is storming
she will grind that freedom
till it runs like sweat down her skin
and when her kids and her men
swing back to her eyes
it will be like waking
from a good, good dream
she thought was real
she will catch her breath and
flush red and cry stupid
but right now it's
*i got all my life to live*
*and i've got all my love to give*
*and i'll survive*
*i will survive*
*hey hey*

## JOHNS WHO DON'T PAY ARE RAPISTS

in my dream it happens
what i feared when i spent nights
in that boston apartment locking
every lock keeping lights on
putting condoms ky baby oil and
wet naps away in a drawer
so i don't have to look at them
unplug those awful air fresheners
plug-ins
a sweet hot cherry stink trying
to hide the scent of cum and latex
peeling back the covers of that bed
like dirty skin, something contaminated
pushing them into a heap on the floor and
sliding to sleep
under a single safe sheet.
but in my dream these men burst in
young and blond like BU students
but with a gun that flashes
on the mirrored walls and
what do they do they throw me
onto the bed and
it is about consent
it is about lines i draw
or lines i watch
get drawn around me
it is a
one hundred dollar
definition of rape
and again,
that mystery consent and
i am confused
i know i should be full of rage
but this feels like just another call,
like just another body pumping at mine
on this same blue bed and
i am raped every day
i am paid well for it

the men kidnap me
they take me through a strange city
and i could break free, i could try
but that gun, small, in his pocket
i am trying to work myself into anger
but i feel so dead in this dream, this dream,
it is only a dream and they take me
to a place that sells ice cream and
sitting on tall stools are three women
i knew in high school and haven't seen since
my heart is still but my brain yells go!
and i grab them and yell help! and
they run with me into a room where
cooks and waitresses crowd around
and i collapse now, tears come
and feelings come they raped me,
i say, they all raped me
cops arrive
tough and anxious to catch the men
who did harm
to such a sweet and small-boned
girl like me
they leave quick in flashing cars
and their promise to return
makes dread and guilt burst
in my belly
because i feel like a liar like
i am telling lies lying
by omission they will return
to a liar-girl crying
on an ice cream parlor floor and say
you weren't raped
no one ever raped you
you're just a whore
who didn't get paid

## DREAM OF AN EX-GIRLFRIEND

last night i dreamt you killed angie dickinson
by stabbing her in the back with a long flat blade.
she lay dead on the basement floor of the apartment
building we lived in and i had to go down there to
get laundry from the dryer and i was frightened, i did
not want to see the blood, the blade sticking out of
her sopping shirt, her eyes staring dead at me
and her mouth frozen open, i know the motive was
properly political but i still can't believe you
killed angie dickinson and just left her lying there,
with perfect hair and makeup growing darker on her
slowly paling face. you killed someone else, too,
and you split town just as i was starting to
get a little scared of you. you left your cat
behind like the last time you left, i hold
him in my arms as i try to explain to
your angry parents why you sped out of
tucson in a sleek green car. i could kill
you for leaving me here in this empty town,
with a cat to take care of and a dead
angie dickinson and a squad of arizona
cops who will find me guilty of murder
and put me away, making me take your rap
like some tragic movie star.

## KATHLEEN

my little sister
got rid of the cockroaches
that lived in her room
by lighting candles
and asking
if they could please respect
her space.
she is smart.
when the men she works with start
throwing laughs like punches over jokes
about homosexuals, she tosses her hair
and says she's queer and the smiles
slide from their faces as they watch
their dreams pop like dead light bulbs.
she is brave.  but not perfect.
this week alone she has eaten
the still flesh of three dead
chickens, they sit in her intestine,
heavy with guilt and karma,
she can feel them.
she is perceptive.
she left a message
on my mother's answering machine:
you can say it was michelle's choice
to stop speaking to you
but all i know is
san francisco's cold,
and she doesn't have a comforter.
one week later, a fifty dollar
check arrives.  she is magic.
and a dancer.  she tells stories
by twisting her limbs like fluid.
if you watch closely the way she leaps
you might learn all her secrets.
my little sister is not a bitch.
she is a scorpio, with a sharp
tail to keep her safe.  she is
as strong as a statue of justice,

but is fooled by her own soft
skin.  my little sister,
she's got the world on her shoulders
and the sun in her eyes, she
is brilliant.  she is like me,
only younger,
and totally different.

## THE ENORMITY OF A BEATEN WOMAN'S BLOOD

beth, who argued with me about
pornography all night, is now
in the midst of a bizarre rant about
wanting to be a fag and kissing gay men
and i am pretending not to hear her
i am talking to peter, who does not
like being in my neighborhood since
that night about a month ago
when a strange man ran up behind him
and brought a fist down heavy on his head.
missing are matthew and eric,
they are kissing beneath a palm tree
in dolores park. soon to be introduced
are the men with the baseball bat
and the prostitute they pick up
and bring to the lot across the street
to beat and stab.
we will meet when her screams
call us from my bedroom, when
she lets us place our shoulders
beneath her arms like crutches
and drag her over pavement
to her mission street apartment.
the wound on her palm will bleed
continuously, like stigmata.
i will feel each warm drop
as they hit my arm and later,
when i try to clean myself,
i will need to use my fingernails
to scrape where it clotted heavy
on my skin. this woman's nose
is a burst of crimson, and peter,
who walks to the side, very conscious
right now of his penis, sees red
trickling from her ears. occasionally,
when she curls over and howls, more
blood falls, splashing my bare feet,
my ankles, even my calves and the color

is identical to the flecks of spraypaint
still clinging to my legs from when i
stenciled the words *ban testosterone*
in the street last week. i will scrub
my skin crazy like a shakespearean witch
before i realize the difference.
and a man whistled as we passed him
steering this broken woman home, he
looked right at her but saw only long
bare legs beneath a short skirt and he whistled
and then there were police and she was enraged
that they show up now, when the knives and bats
and cocks have been packed back into the truck
and hurried away and she says
*you don't give a fuck about prostitutes like me*
she makes it very clear that she wants them to
return to the flashing cars they abandoned
so hastily on the curb, doors flung open and
radios spewing static. they come upon her quickly
and from behind, perhaps the way the last group
of men did they pull her away from us and one
grabs me and keeps me in the same exact hold
the man who queerbashed me in tucson did,
his beefy arms slid beneath my own twin twigs
so that my hands grow pale and numb
and i think i will never be able to
write about this, will never be able to convey
the enormity of a beaten woman's blood
staining your skin or a policeman's rough
arms bruising it. in fact, at that moment
i don't think i will write anymore, ever,
and i will never leave my house, or,
more specifically, my room, or, more
specifically, my bed, i think i will
just sleep for a few weeks because
this whole scene has been a little
draining, this night, these past
weeks, the last few years and
it is hard to get past the fact
that there are some men who tried

to kill a woman tonight, they are
in my city somewhere, probably laughing
about it, probably high from it,
driving recklessly and getting her blood
on the upholstery by the careless way
they toss their weapons and how can i end this,
this just goes on and on the way their lives do,
the way her life does, the bleeding woman
who shouted *thank you* as the cops
stuffed her into their car,
the bleeding woman whose blood
forms a trail which leads to my house,
which i follow like bread crumbs.

## HOW I LOST MY POETRY

there is something scary
about a man with a gun.
this one i can see move towards me,
with purpose, with weapons
one, on his hip, like a warning
and one in his hands, like Too Late
and as he gets closer i realize
he can do anything to me,
he can use that stick
any way he wants
and i wonder,
will it be my head, my knees,
my stomach, face, shoulder
his arms rise as he approaches but
i do not i will not move i
am blocking traffic, planted
like a stop sign before
a shiny red car
and the angry man inside
has gotten so close
his bumper touches my knee
and i think that maybe
this man can do anything, too,
he is yelling, he is threatening and
i am wondering how far
he is going to take it when
the other, with the weapons
and riot gear
(all this, i think,
for a bunch of skinny
queers?)
brings that baton down
on my chest and i
am shocked,
there is something inside me
that will not accept that
someone can come up to me
and hit me with a stick

and it is legal,
i am outraged, he didn't even
speak, didn't even ask me to move
i take the book i hold in my hands
a book of poems, all from my
own head, my own heart my own pen
and i whip them at his head and
that baton comes down on my chest
again and i fall backwards
into the arms of angry dykes who
make sure i'm ok as they shriek
at the cop, the cop whose skin
and features are asian like
the skin and feature
of those people the cops
shoved into camps during that war
Whose Side Are You On i scream
and laugh
at myself
at this surreal place
where a lesbian cop
threatens us for fighting
for her rights and
black men wear the uniform
white men wore as they beat
his people the way
he
is beating mine.
and they won't return my poems,
Evidence, they say, Assault, Arrest
i watch as they read them,
standing in a circle, looking down
on the words of my life like
they could get back their own souls
by kidnapping mine
Keep It, i say as they
laugh and flip the page.
Keep It.
there's more of me
where that came from.

## CRABS ARE NO BIG DEAL

i don't know which body
the crab crawled off of
tiny, grey and hard it
lodged itself in the jungle
of my crotch, multiplying
slowly, feasting on blood or
flakes of dead skin, whatever
parasites prefer. i panicked,
i said That's It, I'm Out
Of This Business, i sat
on the toilet crying, feeling
diseased, plucking occupied
pubic hairs and dropping
them into the bowl where
they tossed like water bugs.

my lover enters with razors
and a can of perfumed foam,
but i prefer soap, i used to
use it to scrape hair from
my legs, my armpits, even
my cunt, yes, i have
experience here, an awful
boyfriend preparing me
for the day my crotch
becomes infested.
we crowd into the
narrow shower
of the flophouse
i'm living in
 provincetown, at the tip
of the cape, the edge
of the world. we shave
our cunts bald as eight
year old girls, me quick
and confident, my lover
slow, scared, barely able to bring
the sharp silver so close

to her clitoris.
when we're done the drain is clogged
with a thick mound of hair
and the tiny struggling bodies of crabs.

my mother had them once, from my
unfaithful father, he blamed them
on her, called her a whore. my mother
told me this story when i was
thirteen, she was sitting on the toilet
like i was when i found them on my own body.
she was drunk
and smoking a cigarette
she said Don't You Ever Spread
Your Legs For Anyone, she was crying.
my friend jessica had them
three times and never from sex,
just sitting around with no underwear.
the horror of finding them nesting
in your crotch, and again, and then
again, i have nightmares like that now.
my friend cathy found a
single purple-grey louse
resting on top of her orange curls
after almost being raped
by a friend of her brother's even
my little sister had them,
from a boyfriend she trusted.
crabs are really
no big deal.

## PETER AND ME

peter and me we were crazy we
were trying to find this thing
danger that we'd heard so much
about we would ride in his car so
drunk so stoned we never crashed
not ever never found that thing
danger not even in the combat
zone where women with veins for bones
stumble down the gutter calling cars
and men stand in clusters
looking at you hard
to find something they might want
we went inside the stores that sold
pictures of women having sex
the way men want them to
back past the magazines and the
paperback books about men
who fuck their daughters and
women who fuck dogs back
past devices black and silver
that people use to hurt each other
and name it sex past the tiny
closets of men jerking off lonely
to stupid movies back to the booth
at the back we cram inside laughing
nervous drunk crazy we slide a
token in and the screen rises just
like in that madonna video which
is a lie of course, there is no
glamour here just an overweight woman
with sickly pale skin she is wearing
a cheap purple teddy and she is
not really dancing just moving
back and forth almost stumbling
she is very drugged her eyes stare
out somewhere above the two way
mirror of the booth peter and me
are in our feet stick to the floor it

is a sick and painful place but
there is no danger here and
we leave the shop in a burst
of energy rushing back out
into the combat zone and i
wonder what he was thinking i
wonder what i was thinking we
were running through boston like
lunatics we were looking for
something to give us a shock we
were looking for a danger stronger
than the danger of our lives
we didn't find it.

## HOW I LIVED MY LIFE IN TUSCON

i was an activist, an amazon, an empowerer of women
i would bring us together to sit on the university lawn,
shirts on the grass beside us, our breasts coloring with sun,
daring the cops to arrest us, daring the courts to tell us
that what we were doing was illegal when my friend matthew
could whip off his shirt and walk down the street whenever he wanted
the sunlight toying with the gold through his nipple and we had
signs, we had chants, we were loud and we passed out flyers,
my face and name on the news each night, in the paper each morning
i would plan these protests and move through them like a young
gloria steinem when the beeper in my pocket would sound its
shrill siren and i would grab matthew, who knew how to drive,
and together we would speed back to my house where those
shaggy grass-stained jeans would be shed for a dress, my
hair would be arranged like a pile of feathers and
i would even put on lipstick because i was a call girl,
a lesbian feminist radical activist prostitute,
the only one in pima county if not the entire state
of arizona and the men whose homes i would visit
would try to place where they knew me from, squinting
their cowboy eyes at me and figuring i was just another
pretty face until one night, as they sit eating meatloaf
with their wives, i appear on the six o'clock news
screaming at a bunch of frat boys, my nipples covered
with electrical tape, a baseball hat hiding my hair, but
*yep, that's her alright, the little whore who faked an orgasm*
*in my bedroom just three nights ago and what do you know,*
*she's one of them goddamn freak of nature lesbians!*
my boss, a very feminine woman named katarina,
says in a nervous twitter over the telephone
*why, i thought that was you, well, what you do on*
*your own time is your business, as long as it's not drugs,*
*does this mean you'll see women?*   katarina, whose neck
is marked with thin rings that you can count like the trunk
of a tree to see how many face-lifts she's had, she would
beep me and i would run, changing costume like a
superhero in an underground comic book, from feminist activist
to southwestern escort and back and i'm not sure

which role is braver, who i'm changing into
and out of and really i'm not changing at all, just
rearranging, hiding my leg hair under garters and
hiding my condoms in the purse i hide in the back seat
of the car, tucson is a hot town where a woman
should be able to take off her shirt, tucson is
a depressed town where a woman should be able to make some money
without selling twelve hours of her time for 48 dollars and a pair
of swollen feet and yeah, it was like having your cake
and trashing it too, or getting the best of both worlds
when no world is best, not in this world anyway,
and it might seem like a contradiction
but if you took the time to look
you'd see they were just two sides
of the same coin and that was how
i lived my life in tucson.

## WHAT I KNOW

don't you know?
don't you know?
when a boy
            hits you
it means he
            likes you.
and he likes me,
this eight-year-old boy
who took my shoulders
who held them against the wall
and made his tongue crawl
into my mouth
like a bad animal.
and he likes me,
this boy on the bicycle who keeps
hitting me he keeps hitting me
he pedals past with his hand out
to clip my head or he flicks
down his kickstand to make me
run and he likes me
this boy who took a stick
and whacked the curve of my
crotch and the girls all giggled,
yeah, he must *really* like you and
it would seem like the prettiest girls
could wear their luck like bruises
because don't you know?
don't you know?
it means they like you
when they fling small rocks
in your direction
it means they like you
when they tug your hair
to make your neck snap back
when they pinch your arm
to make your skin glow red
it means they like you,
judy blume said so, too,

it's in her books it's in
a lot of books it's in
their eyes as their hands
are reaching out for you,
that look of love, you've
seen it in your father's eyes
as his own hands reached out
for your mother and he likes her,
he even loves her, don't you know?
they just sometimes
have a hard time
showing it, these boys,
these silly
        silly
                boys, when
they hit you
                it means
they like you.
don't you know?

## BUS STORY

listen.
i have a dirty mind.
i was on the bus and
there was this man and
on his lap was a young girl and
it was the way his hands touched
her waist, familiar, like a secret exposed,
and then he bounced his knee and he laughed
it was the way he laughed, intimate, i
looked away with a blush, feeling
like i had stumbled upon lovers but he
had caught my eye and
his look was defiant, it dared me, and again that
laugh, and the bounce of his knee, and her voice,
the high pitch of a child but straining down, reaching
for the lipstick low of a woman's, and my
stomach lurched with the braking of the bus
and i looked back as i left and his eyes caged hers and
his hand was in her ponytail and hers, small, a
pale starfish touching his chest and
i cannot do anything, his wet
laugh shoves me from the bus, i stand in a
tornado of exhaust, choking, my imagination
wild, pummeling my dirty mind with scenes i
might remember but won't let myself see, the bus
is gone now, the girl is gone and the man's
glare sticks to me like a third eye, there are things
i know that others don't know and there are things
i see that you can't see
my mind
a secret decoder an open wound a trap
with jaws that spring on the tender ankles
of young girls, girls i can't save, i turn
down the street and walk i have somewhere to go i
have things i have to do my mind is dirty enough
without the dirty hurt of a young girl's secret
i've got my own secrets, do you understand, i've got
my own secrets.

## RIGHT WHERE YOU SHOULD BE

if she had come to you like a gypsy,
if she had spread it before you like cards,
would you have surrounded your bed
with a dozen black candles
and tried to rub the lines from your palms?
no. you would have lied still and waited for it
to hit you like a wave. you could not have missed
the ride through texas, stoned, sylvia plath on your lap
and your whole self pressed up against the glass, the squeeze
of her hand pulling you away from the shriveled winter desert.
and the bedroom you spraypainted gold with a sundress tied
hopelessly around your nose and mouth. the mexico-bound hippies
who stayed on your floor for a week would laugh
when you blew gold snot from your nose and you worried,
imagining your life span stunted 10 or 15 years.
but that room, the tucson sun lit the paint and made it glow,
and you lived there, beneath the ceiling you stenciled with stars
and half-moons and sometimes
she would get stingy with her life
and would tend to herself like a lover and
you would watch jealously as she rubbed her skin
with aloe from the backyard
and you would be jealous when you fought
and she would take the car to the desert
to be alone with the saguaros while you
were left to wander the dusty city,
finding solitude in the lot behind a frat house
where you would smoke cigarettes and write
in the diary she will later read because she can't ask you
how you feel but she needs to know. hold on.
stop. don't let nostalgia knock you down.
when you split up she will have a boyfriend
who will inevitably make her pregnant, but you will have
a city full of women who have little need for boys.
she will keep the cat who slept with his slinky body
curled to the curve of your belly, but you will get
her best friend, he thinks she's lost her mind.
she will get the car you bought and tried to learn to drive.

she will get the futon, paid for with your mother's money.
she will get the two hundred dollar tent you meant to camp in.
she will get tucson, that ghost town, and all the heat
her dry skin can take.
you will get a duffle bag full of clothing you're not sure you like,
a sleeping bag
and a pillow stolen from a cape cod motel. stop.
don't be bitter. and don't go to nightclubs.
you'll never find a worthy lover there.
learn from your mistakes: the one who hung pictures of supermodels
above her bed like some psychotic adolescent - cindy,
naomi, tatiana, claudia, iman, they
watched with smoldering eyes and pouting lips
as she wrapped her legs around you.
and the one who danced like you were lovers already,
how she took your hand like it was a leash,
pulled you into the bathroom and kissed you exactly how
you wanted to be kissed. you thought the boy on her couch
was a fag. you thought the men's clothes in the closet
were hers. stop. when you realize
how long it's been since you have felt the body
of a new woman beside you, do not let it depress you.
let it inspire you.
you might wonder where 13 months of monogamy has gotten you.
you might go back to the beginning before you thought
you loved her, when you went home with someone else.
you were so brave. the woman was older and exciting
but in the morning her sleeping weight made your legs fall asleep.
and you wished it had never happened. stop. never regret anything.
if you had let her buy your love with breakfast and drink tickets
where would you be right now? you can't even imagine.
you are right where you should be.
now act like it.

## WHAT HAPPENED

this is what happened:
the kitchen was pale green
sea green and
i am drowning.

this is what happened:
i was bending over
blood rushed to my face and
i am fainting.

this is what happened:
my skirt was up
my ass was bare and
i am shaking.

this is what happened:
the man was behind me
he was my father and
i don't know what happened.

## DYSFUNCTIONAL LOVE POEM FOR ALI

i just want to self-destruct with her,
to spark a whiskey fuse and watch it blow,
suck ashes in like air and hug her blistered skin
because i know how nothing binds like trauma
and highways
and we never did make it to reno,
my finger tracing a sad path on the atlas
from the desert to the ocean to a
hunting ground on the san andreas fault
to a lake on a golf course in daly city to
the safeway parking lot on market street
where we sit trading tragedies like damp matches
and i just want to take your hand and
run to the nearest bar but i know all
the fancy words they have for that so
let's just talk,
you've got a story about a girl for
every corner in san francisco, dramatic
ones like lying in the rain threatening
to shave a heavy head if you leave, dramatic
like the offer never made to the woman
whose name you never even knew,
you were going to ask her to skip town
with you and god! i think shit like that
is so romantic, if i had known
that cleaning up my act would cost me
crash and burn passion with a woman like you
i would've torn at my scabs with my teeth
and left a stinking trail of blood
for you to find me.
and why am i being greedy?
i've got a mark on my neck
the size of texas and it came from
your sweet teeth, i've got a night
spent under the plastic stars on your ceiling,
i've got you in my mind,
your breath on my body
and the words you said,

*a gentle woman*
from your lips maybe not a blessing
but i will eat it anyway
and like how it feels in my belly.
the very next day i get my period
with a red hormone rush that makes me cry
while reading your poetry on the 24 bus
your poetry that makes mine look like cartoons,
like the rat gnawing on my bone is just
mickey mouse's fat hand giving me a slap
and it's that desperate feeling, i've had it before,
like wanting to protect a woman from
everything that's already happened to her,
like wanting to work the first man you see
into a bloody fucking mess because
you know he's hurt some woman somewhere
at some point in his life and remember,
i've got my period and i'm dizzy
from hormones and the passion
of her poetry and i stumble by the
cafe she works at and embarrass
myself further by telling her one more time
how much i like her, just to remind her
it is somewhat more than she likes me
but she gives me a hug when i leave
and i feel better today, cramps
and hormones under control and
the book of her poetry stuffed
in my bag, buzzing like a beehive
if i get too close.

# TRIPPING ON LABIA

Mass Extinction Press
1994

## THE LOVE FOR A MOTHER IS A TOUGH, TOUGH LOVE

i talked to my mother today,
her voice was thick with sleep
and cigarettes. i could
almost smell that house
and the smoke that soaked
my clothes, the television glow
spilling over worn plaid white trash
couch and coffee table stained
with waxy rings from sweating glasses
of coke, the stale stink of homemade
knitted afghans wrapped around
sweaty feet, the shoes, the soft white
nurses' shoes, dirty with hospital germs.
but wait, wrong house, she is
lifting my voice to her ear in a new house
without holes in walls, without daughters
without even a room for daughters
should they repent and return,
should the patriarch die.
she wants to know if i'm happy
but she does not want to know
what is making me happy.
dark bars where i get drunk on words
*i am writing,* i say, *i have a new book*
and the line becomes this void filled with her fear,
what fucked up thing has happened now
to pull words from my pen, she doesn't want
to know and the line is this void filled
with anger i will never express,
thinking about the woman i loved for a year,
we crisscrossed the country three times together.
i've been without her for four months
and my mother, she doesn't ask
she has never even asked.
and *i'm in love,* i tell her,
*that's why i am happy.*
i'm in love every day
every day with someone new

i'm in love with this whole city,
like the love was there first
and these women just make me
want to share it, and women,
yes, women, and sometimes it feels
like they could be in love too.
they offer me their tongues
tucked in the red velvet boxes of
their mouths and i am in love,
i tell her (leaving out the details).
*that's nice, dear.*
nights spent in a love
that yields her no grandchildren
making as much sense
as a job that yields no pay.
but i'm an activist. *ma,*
*it's volunteer work, it feeds my soul.*
work is drudgery
and she works, she works 7-3
she works 3-11
she works 11-7
till her nose becomes blind to the smell
of shit and living too long, she goes home
to her home, the home she owns, she
is a homeowner, with brand new furniture
cheap green velvet, they are for show
and holidays and guests who can sit
with their asses tightly clenched.
and all those thick-haired dolls with careful
porcelain faces tucked cutely into curios
and her animals, the cat she tore
the claws from, the dog barking
from its fenced in pantry pen.
living things are such a responsibility,
they are so hard to control, but she tries.
and i love her, i love her
i love her like a mother loves a daughter
who is moving in the wrong direction,
hanging out with the wrong crowd,
going with a guy you know is just no good.

i love her with a love big enough to hold every hurt
every time she did me wrong,
and the betrayal,
the big one like the atom bomb, the one
that worked us into ground zero like
we're living in nevada now, out in the desert
and every time i get too close i fear contamination
and i love her, so i weld words into instruments
trying to pry the crack in her heart
but they're too big, clumsy to make her angry
or too small, sliding from my fingers into that place
where she keeps everything she never wants to see
(her life). and i love her, she is dying a slow,
slow death that will have taken her whole life to reach
in that house, with her cigarettes, her television,
her hamburger helper and her husband.
and i love her.

## FOR MY NANA

i liked this boy adam
with long hair and black eyeliner
and he was all i could think about
when i took my grandmother to boston
for radiation treatments.
they were zapping her lungs nuclear
and i was sitting in the waiting room
with ginger ale and national geographic
and hidden hickeys, and you could hear
the machine buzz and hum as it
spit out nuclear stripes and isn't
cancer caused by radiation in the first place?
all that atomic 1950's air they were making
out in nevada worked its way to boston and
into my nana's lungs and now they've got her
drinking these uranium cocktails so that
her sink is full of wet hairs and later,
in the hospital cafeteria over rubbery hot dogs
and coffee she says *let's have a cigarette together,*
*this will be your last one, ok? you inhale?*
*don't inhale, i never inhale.*
this woman
whose judas cells are killing her
she tells me not to sit on the toilet
cause i might get aids and not to
put my lips on the drinking fountain
cause i could get hepatitis.
my grandmother died
with her eyebrows drawn perfect,
just as she'd requested. she died before
my boyfriends stopped looking like girls and
started being girls, before she could hate
me for being her queer aquarius granddaughter,
same zodiac sign as her, and did you know
that some cultures kill all the february babies
because their little bodies have so much bad magic?
she had psychic dreams, my grandmother, she knew
each symbol had a number and she'd play the

lottery and win a hundred bucks and she loved
my cousin brian, the connecticut hairdresser
with a joan crawford fixation, so who knows,
maybe she would have loved my hairy armpits
the way i loved how she pin-curled her hair tight
before it all fell out and she began hiding
her baldness with eva gabor wigs,
and i never visited her grave except that one time
my mother dragged me to the cemetery with a
poinsettia for christmas, there was nothing there
but a flat copper plaque, half covered with snow
and a group of groundskeepers
who sexually harassed my mom on the
way back to the car. nana, if reincarnation
is true, you are a six-year-old child somewhere
on this planet. i hope your parents treat you good,
i hope you have enough to eat and a best friend
all your own, i hope you don't hate school too much
or maybe i hope you hate it a lot, i hope you
were born in february again, i hope you came back new.

## GO KISS GO

i've got a two-day-old kiss and
i'm afraid it's getting stale, i'm
trying to keep it covered, keep it
fresh, don't know when the next batch
is coming. got an ache in my heart
from this two-day-old kiss, it's pretty
heavy for something that isn't even
there, it likes to jump from my ribs
like a high dive and go swimming in
my stomach, it likes to slide deep
down there, yeah there, you know where
and do a little tap dance, it likes to
catch a ride on my bloodstream up to
my ears, make them burn, make me sweat
a little, gets a little bossy, a little
greedy, kicks my brain out like it owns
the place, making my head swell full
with this two-day-old kiss which isn't
even anything, making me fuck up a lot
in work sayin' sorry, sorry, sorry, i forgot
to do that, sorry i did that wrong, sorry
i just forgot i was here, i just went
somewhere else for a minute. i just
got kissed two days ago and you know
that clock is ticking.

# THIS DOESN'T HAPPEN OFTEN

drunk
and i did it on purpose cuz i don't have
to work in the morning, it's thanksgiving and
america will be spending the afternoon fisting a turkey.
listen
i've heard your poetry and i know that you're
probably saying intelligent things, but i can't
listen, i'm too busy freaking myself out by
imagining you sucking my nipple, my lips
on your face and my hands in your hair.
girl
please come back to san francisco real soon
i need your tongue on my earlobe to remind me
who i am, i got a fag friend telling me it's
not dysfunction, it's just about being human.
please
don't read my poetry, if you want to touch
my mind just look at my eyes, they're my brain reaching
out for reality like a country girl with big dreams,
let me be frank: the thought of your penis doesn't
make me spazz so much right now, i wouldn't
put it in my mouth but maybe i would touch it.
honestly
i thought you'd invite me over, thought you'd want
some company for the walk home, cold and windy like i'm
back in boston again, not in california with plastic suns
and palm trees, thought i'd make that whiskey work for me.
so
i'm heading home with embarrassing telephone fantasies,
your voice on my answering machine like a woman
and if you must know, midnight cab rides are my preferred
method of transportation, i could be at your place before you
can say the word bisexual and find it in the
dictionary, if you don't already know.
forget
the asshole things he said, like henry miller and, well,
that's all really, except for that poem where he gets
angry at that girl for not fucking him. honey,

don't you know, never bed a writer, but when you've
seen his soul on paper, it's his body that's intriguing.
create
a conversation in your drunken bus-bored head like
*i thought you didn't like boys* and then something like
*i don't expect for political poets with long hair and*
*the same zodiac sign as me.* relax. there'll be other
nights, other hormonal cycles and whiskey sours,
relax girl, get it together.

## HELL IS A STATE SCHOOL

college was a big dream
of a clandestine lesbian affair,
groping for wet spaces in a dorm room
beneath platonic blankets and quiet
not to wake my sleeping homophobe
roommate....
it didn't quite happen like that
i think my boyfriend
scared the girls away and
my roommate's bed was always full
of her shirtless steady, sweating
the air into a thick and boozy
man stink and what was i thinking,
coming to school in this place that
every intelligent person leaves at 18.
the campus
is just a high school
with a history requirement
that is flying through greece
like sappho never happened
and a professor who makes
the word *democracy*
sound magnificent as he
neglects to mention things
i find important, like
cleopatra not having
a clitoris and a few
million women murdered
for being witches, widows
and whores, but that's old news
in this town, where their own
burnt women
are a tourist celebration
complete with an Official Witch
who blesses the football team
every autumn and a police squad
wearing patches of broom-straddling
hags and my french teacher tells me

clarence thomas would not have been a
problem in paris, women like sex there,
and psych 101 is a dark room with
films rolling out of the 60's, white men
testing a black woman's sanity
by making her count backwards
and recite a long list of presidents
and if it wasn't for my women's studies class,
if it wasn't for abortion rights,
domestic violence, white privilege and
*the joy luck club*, if it wasn't for
that red-faced professor and the
homophobia project that pulled her
from the closet but left me stranded
in boyfriendland with mr. insecurity
asking each day did i wear makeup,
a tight dress, a bra, did i see
any good-looking guys and you
swear my penis isn't too small?
if it wasn't for my carnivorous
teeth i would have starved sick like
my vegetarian friend, wasting away
slowly with a bagel and an unpunched
meal card and each night someone pulls
the fire alarm, sending a pajamaed dormitory
onto the frozen new england dirt for two early
hours till all the firemen leave and
each night the overweight girls
in the room next door play rap music
and scream and let me get this right:
i am paying this institution
to tell me what to know
to tell me which facts are important
and in need of a bed
in my overcrowded head,
and i worked all year
at a shitty office job
to buy these books full of white men
and lies and this white block of a dorm room
because i thought it would be charming

like a katherine hepburn movie,
like the summer camp i never got to go to
and if it wasn't for that one lipstick lesbian
and the drag bar in the town next door
i might've drowned in my own tears that year,
that string of winter months
when i got my education.

## THIS IS ABOUT KARMA
for keri

i see you haunting your doorways
like a naked ghost, gagging on your
toothbrush in your bathroom in your
messy house with fruit flies in the sink
and cats in the closet. it must be cold
in boston, like that snowstorm that
knocked the power out and left us
dressing in the dark, listen, best friend
of my mean old lover, you had the
clearest blue eyes of all you blue-eyed
blue-blooded children and how your tall
bones stuck up for me when i was drunk
on confusion and fear of a family whirling
down a hole like a tub of dirty bathwater,
it was like i had battered woman's syndrome
or something, trapped in her headlights
like a bony animal, trapped in my life
desperate but not yet brave enough
to gnaw off my paw, and keri, i wish
i hit her with the truth like a pie in the face
because she really did read your diary
and then laugh at your writings
with her boyfriend, she really did plot
to sleep with your grungy ex-lover, i heard
her call him with a sexy voice on and
i guess i was there too, going along for
the ride, and i'm sorry, i'm trying to clean up
my karma and i'm afraid those cramps are
my conscience rotting in my gut
like a herd of hamburger, and i hope that
you are well and that that job rockets you
into the desert with your wise-eyed cats
and your shaman boyfriend picking
futures out of dictionaries and maybe
when i learn how to drive i'll come
park my car in your dusty driveway,
eat your stew and tortillas and your

sweet boiled beet, read your tarot cards
and smoke a cigarette, but for now i'm stuck
in the city, hopping cafes like boxcars,
my ears full of other people's words
and remember how you'd laugh at all those
boston poets, you got a mean streak girl,
and a real loud laugh, and now every time
i hear bad poetry i think of all your tangled
hair, i think of you quite often.

## FAKE DUCK/BAD TRIP

before it got bad
we were hanging with the ducks
in golden gate park, the ducks
that are on those stamps, their shiny green
heads so much prettier in person
and they keep the seagulls so clean here too,
not like those grimy oil-slicked birds
shitting all over my porch in provincetown.
but the ducks, watch them do their
mating dance, stretch that neck to heaven,
beat a wet chest with feathers
and scream: *let me tell you this:*
you've got to treat every single animal
the way you'd want to be treated,
do you understand? it's simple,
no cages, no leashes, no dead flesh
disguised as food.
on the bus
my eyes can't focus
everything is a blur
but your cherubic face,
and don't you feel bad for
all our adolescent enemies?
it's so obvious now that
they've all been sexually abused.
remember
when we were watching the ducks?
i said *this shit isn't working*
and stuffed more green brownie
into my mouth, and look,
there's a cop, *mmmmm, mmmmm,*
*what a yummy brownie,*
*just eating a brownie, officer,*
*mmmmm, mmmmm.*
you know,
i think i ate too much,
i think they take awhile
to kick in.

i think
there is no such thing as time
and the way you swing your arms
when you walk
is responsible for the way that man
is scratching his ear.
don't ask me how i know this, but it's true
and i'm glad you're not like me
someone's got to make sure we can
cross the streets safely
and get to the vegetarian restaurant
halfway across town. wow,
you really know your way around
san francisco, wow, i can't believe
i'm fucking living in san francisco,
how the hell did i end up here?
and this place serves fake meat,
yes,
fake meat and i don't know, what does that mean?
my friend ate here, she recommended the duck,
i was going to have the duck, fake duck,
what the fuck is fake duck? either it's duck
or it's not, and if it's not duck, what is it?
why are we pretending to eat meat, where the fuck
are we and why can't i move my legs, why
has the waitress checked back with us three times
to make sure we want what we ordered, does she know
i'm fucked up, am i making a scene? it's just that
i don't want to eat a duck, i like ducks,
those green-headed ducks with their wings
spread wide, does the fake duck come with
fake wings, can we just go,
can you pay for this i have money in my
pocket but i just can't deal with moving
my hand, i just can't handle it, i'm
glad you understand, you're so nice, peter,
such a nice person, i'm so glad
you're my best friend. holy shit,
it just hit me how fucked up my
ex-girlfriend is. how could i have

stayed with her for a whole fucking
year? oh my god, i must really be
screwed up. i must need therapy,
do you think i need therapy? my life is
such a wreck, i was thinking everything
was great. but really it sucks, maybe i should
put myself in a hospital or something and
why does the waitress keep bringing us all
these different sauces, this one looks like poop,
where's the duck sauce, duck sauce, what is it
with fucking ducks today
i've got to go home.

## WE ARE GIRLS
for heather

we do not touch.
we are girls.
our nipples are jellybeans,
they are iron, they are
the steel tips of the boot
that is our body, they are fuses
and that is not always bad.
we do not touch.
we are girls.
our cunts are caves,
we turn each other inside out
to walk inside, invite each other in,
leave wet footprints on our bones,
have a house party, have a
treasure hunt because they say
they say
they say
there is something inside us girls
and we mean to find it, we
are oceans, deep as oceans
we are and it gets darker the deeper,
so dark we grow lights for eyes like
those sand-belly fish,
they are girls too
swimming in the shipwrecks in
the pieces of the past, broken
on coral, slick with sea.
you do not know what is down there,
you do not know.
we do not touch.
we are girls.
with an extra heart pumping double
we have too much blood
in our bodies
sometimes
we drain, we
are drained.

our guardian angels
are hiding switchblades
in their feathers.
those wings are muscle,
watch out.
they wait
until the sun can't hear
and whisper sweet subversions
into our ears,
they are girls too.
and we do not touch,
we shoot fear into our veins
like vaccination.
fear fighting fear, this
is how we live, immune,
we have to be immune,
we are girls.
(and sometimes we touch like
a dream coming back, that dark
and sleeping void and you
remember, it is not empty and
safe, we are not safe and
our bodies know that,
every cell has evolved, they
grow towards pleasure always,
they adapt.
and if you feed them only pain, well,
they adapt.)
and we are girls,
sometimes our voices are fingers, they
negate the need for hands,
when our words wrap like bone,
when our words, squeezed forever
beneath too much, too hot, too hurt,
burst like diamonds from coal
and cut scratches through the glass
you live in, you were warned.
we are girls.
and if we could find
the hand that feeds us

we'd bite, but we haven't
been fed in so, so long
and we are hungry
and throwing a piece of meat
into the ghetto
you built us into
is not enough.
we have been hungry forever:
we were born hungry
through that open hungry mouth we
were born from our mothers' hunger, we are
hunger birthing hunger birthing hunger
we grind our teeth in our sleep
we are girls.
and sometimes we can crawl
into each other like caves, we
can curl, we can sleep,
we are girls.

## I USED TO BE STRAIGHT

i'm lighting votive candles
for the straight girls of america
lying on mattresses in their boyfriends'
loft apartments, posing naked for
their brilliant artist boyfriends, or otherwise
inspiring them to new levels of straight boy
genius, smoking cigarettes with each other
as they bitch about their sadly
tortured boyfriends, so proud
they've got a boy to bitch about.
i'm lighting votive candles
for the straight girls of america
because they'll never get the oscars
they deserve. and every now and then
i catch my ghost astride a cock that wasn't
even paying, hearing him ask
*do you ever think of being with a woman ?*
and i'd seen enough pornography to
know the proper answer to send him
sifting through his brain like a little
black book, landing on the one
who used to watch her roommate
masturbate in boarding school.
she said i reminded her of
the mother she never met,
and i fell in love with her on
railroad tracks wishing he'd go away,
fell in love with her in his bedroom
wishing i was any place else
and she apologized for her body
when she saw my cunt as bare
as a brand, apologized like she hadn't
been paying attention and let some
important lesson pass her by.
and give me insults, give me
economic discrimination, give me
the darkened parking lot of a
windowless queer bar, give me

fleets of bigots and books banned
in libraries across america, feed the world
with lies about my life and plop a second
helping of oppression on my plate
and thank you for not making me straight.
straight girls of america, i am lighting
votive candles for your ignored and
misused clitorises, burning my draft card
for the war between the sexes,
but will be your soldier still.
i will escort you to abortionists
till the end of time, my bible-bruised
body braced against the door, i will
be joan of arc for you, madonna
and janet jackson, the voices in my head
pushing me ever into battle.
straight girls of america, i am
lighting votive candles in the church
of self-righteous condescension.
but sisters,
i've been there.

## TRICK POEM #2

entering his house
gracelessly as he
entered me, tripping
on carpet like labia.
the way he pulled at
my vulva like a thick
skinned grapefruit
*let me*, and i parted
flesh for the roll
of bills on his wife's
dresser. the cock that
pushed quick into that
red room and knocked
my eggs all loose.
*easy*, i said, my girl
hands on his thick
hips, his copper-
mine hands on the
bed by my head, his
green socks hanging
on his ankles, his
silver crewcut, his
pot belly slapping
into me, his voice
*all the way or no*
*pay.*

# HEARTBREAK CIGARETTES

borrowed time press
1995

...but i owe my life to these very imperfections,
my fistful of desires.
You could call it restraint or you could call it a chokehold.
You could call it common courtesy or you could call it
a basketful of lies.  You could call me
the sister of Icarus or the village idiot or a woman scorned
and i wouldn't mind.
What's a warm-blooded animal to do
among all you
so cool?

- Eli Coppola

## MY HEART

i got a tattoo in tucson
from a guy named rembrandt,
the needle burned like fire melted and
a friend named jessica held my hand,
telling me stories about children
throwing starfish to the ocean.
i branded the crescent of my nails
to her palm and when she left i
tore fistfuls of fur from the stuffed cat they
kept for such purpose.
i tattooed my heart above
my heart and back in san
francisco ali worries i'll think forever
about the woman who broke it but
this heart's mine.
rembrandt looks like
my stepfather that same i'm old
but cool tough but
sensitive i treat women right but
go to tit bars cause i like
to see them shake it same
hulk hogan mustache curving
down his lips i remember my
stepfather's sage tattoo advice he said
once you got it it's a
distinguishing mark,
easier for the cops to find you, outlaw
yet fine upstanding father-
figure.
the notches on rembrandt's belt made me
uneasy but i thought it was
the emblem for a metal band with
sexist videos and andy who did
the piercings, nineteen-year-old fag
sick of sucking tucson dust said
it's the logo for some white
supremacist group.
someone said do you

think all that bad energy sunk
to your skin with the red
and black ink and i said no,
this heart's mine.

## ON LEARNING MY LOVER WAS A WHORE
## OR IT'S ALL HER FAULT

oh is that all?
the way she had prepared me i
was thinking AIDS or cancer or
maybe she was a straight girl
playing a joke on me
my imagination gets wild,
sometimes.
i had just finished reading
that sex work anthology, the
irony, no wonder she'd
been so anxious to read it.
i thought
this is so cool,
my girlfriend's a prostitute,
i felt so radical and
once i knew i could hang out
at her house and watch her wait
for the telephone to ring,
hear her talk to them in a
breathy female voice she
never used with me
(i was glad)
i would kiss her as she
dragged her purse out the door
leaving my lips tasting of
clinique and paloma picasso
and at night she
would make me feel like refuge,
sliding up beside me in our girly-girl bed
she had boyfriends before me,
not one of them she told.
they all thought she was a spoiled
trust fund bitch
and she was,
but she worked, too.
i started thinking
it's not fair,

how she pays for everything
takes me to cape cod
to watch weekend waves shape the sand
buys expensive wine, lobster,
raw things in shells that look like
vulva and then
i started thinking
it's not fair
how i work so much
feet sore from scuttling like a roach
across the floor of that middle eastern
restaurant my mustached bosses
sexually harassing me in
body language i just couldn't shut up.
when i told her i
wanted a job she
laughed, said
remember when we picked up
that pretty long-haired boy
how the sight of his dick gave me
nausea and diarrhea both so
i didn't know which end to stick in
the backed-up toilet of
his father's beach hotel,
i just locked myself in
the bathroom and cried that's
different i said.

i got
a tube of lipstick got
high heel shoes got
a pocketbook of condoms a
tight black dress i
got my first call i
flew there on tequila and
taxi feeling
dangerous like some
new york city fantasy like
anais nin he
was old, pouchy as droopy dog

smoking virginia slims like an
aging queen and
name dropping publishing moguls i
couldn't care less.
how easy it was except
for the teddy bear in
the rocking chair he
kept calling it fatso said
i hope you're not shy said
fatso likes to watch so
i spent the hour paranoid of
a video camera hidden in
the stuffing of fatso's
belly.  it was over
so quick, out front of his house in
the hip part of town i waited
for my cab and hid from friends
who would want to know why
i was dressed like a whore.
i looked for the line i thought
i'd crossed but i couldn't
find it anywhere i was
ok i didn't feel desperate or
even dirty it was the
easiest hundred dollars it
opened the world like
a natural disaster it
sailed me home,
a flying green carpet.

## THAT LOOK

i had heard stories
from women who'd been there
how the look of fear in a man's eye
could be like drugs. laura
who'd chased men away in her
big black boots swore by it like
morning coffee her long long hair
pulled them to her flies until she
had an aerosol can full of attitude she
pulled a blade on an off duty cop once,
held it to his throat and said let's go
muthafucka like she thought she was in
a movie or something and i had heard
how you can watch their fear like a sliver
of the moon growing full and it had always
been there like drugs i had heard addictive and
kym beat up a man with her fists once, broad
daylight and everyone just stood there
women in their windows men in a circle and
no one made a move to help him thank you
saint kitty of the city streets she sent his
bank deposits flying pieces of money everywhere he
had wanted to see her tits and she had made him
run and i had heard it could be like drugs or
candy something sweet something that
makes you smile and to see their fear come out it's
like midwifing your own birth making
the frat boy that attacked your friend cry with only
the threat of your voice, we did that, bandanas
tied around our faces like amazon cowgirls and
the words coming out of our mouths took shape
and stood beside us in his bedroom he
crying and that look it sent me running
down his hallway choking on joy it is like
wine but bigger it is like falling in love
and it grows, one sent running down a beach
for staring one sent running from a
restaurant dinner under his arm because

we didn't care what he thought about two
girls kissing and all the ones left standing
on the sidewalk with their mouths open and
their eyes their eyes open and it's easy,
you just let you fear slide back like
medicine and keep your eyes open don't
let them flicker catch their eyes hold
them tight as bone let your tongue
turn twisters let your palms fly like
angels just hold those two eyes still
and watch the moon come out.

## FIVE REASONS WHY I MAY DIE OF CANCER

my mother hoarded cigarettes
when i was living in her womb.
six a day, she sucked them down
like ritual and i developed
a taste at thirteen
for looking tough with a chainlink
belt, black lace gloves with
amputated fingers and a box
of marlboros, my parents
never knew, i was already so
smoke-soaked from swimming
through their secondhand breath,
white trash rappucinis preparing
their daughters for this toxic world,
this is how humans evolve.
i quit at eighteen, making exceptions
for the occasional broken heart
or heated conversation, but those vines
that grew black in my lungs like
a fifth grade science textbook,
i imagine them hanging on,
tough as kudzu, and cancer,
that tarzan, swinging through the cells.
i was born with a birthmark
bumpy and erupting like
a sick volcano on the back of my head.
in salem or europe
i'd have been burnt or drowned but
here they knocked me out and
sliced it off for fear of
melanoma but it's like
cancer's left its tag
and the bricks of my body
and it is looking for a way
to slip inside those high school years
didn't help, when *dead girl*
was my fashion statement,
sunless skin and black hair dye

that i just read in *ms.* magazine
contains coal-tar that
makes the cells in your lymph nodes
go wild and the playground
where i practiced my cheerleading,
hands grubby from useless cartwheels,
it stunk a stink that clung
to every part of you
and now we learn
it was built on a toxic waste dump.
there is a clump of radiation
nesting in my thyroid cuz
thyroids like iodine and
when i was eight i'd get these
pains in my abdomen and the doctors
couldn't figure out what it was about,
they stuck fingers up my butt,
drew so much blood i've got
way cool track marks and
probably it was psychological because
i hated my parents but
they had to be sure,
they shot me up full of radioactive iodine,
some nuclear power-plant waste product
and the nurse said your mouth
will taste like copper,
just like the soldier who said it was
like sucking on a penny when he
walked straight into that pink nevada cloud,
they said my kidney is shaped like a horseshoe
and that was the end of that.
this is more than enough
i cannot begin to think of things
like pesticides, saccharin,
and the five-year-old boy
who died at a barbeque
from too much Deep Woods Off.
this world
is so dangerous
it makes me hear
my body ticking.

## EMOTIONAL MASOCHISM OR
## NEW AGE MESSAGE FROM BEYOND?

i spent all afternoon telling
the woman that i love that
she should take that terrible risk and
tell our best friend exactly how
she feels about her.

i read in a book about a woman's
after death experience when she learned
that we choose our entire destiny
before we are born.

the sun is going down on
7th and market giving all
the homeless crackheads a sunset
glow of health i am listening
to michelle shocked and smoking
p.c. cigarettes i am searching
for the lesson i
am trying to teach myself.

## PEOPLE I'VE LOST

twelve dozen of my
self, all with different
hairdos.

a homeless poet reading squinty
loud from scraps of trash i
bought him a notebook but
he was gone.

an arizona woman and the kids i
helped save from her husband's greasy
dick, five hundred dollar bank account
and i hope she's far away.

the orange-haired lady from
ireland stinking from weeks of
sundaes we had cold sprained
wrists from frozen tubs of cream and
i didn't know i wanted to kiss her.

my old lover's brother steven held
hostage in his parent's barbie
dream house, cincinnatti ohio she's
got his number in her mouth with
all those teeth.

my mother but not the one
mainlining disneyworld i
know where to find that one i
lost the one lactating promise while
i sucked on a bottle of similac
was looking for a while and then
i stopped.

## ANOTHER DAY AT WORK

he said
he said sorry
hope i didn't
offend you
calling that
woman
a cunt
sorry
and i say
well
it's just that
hearing a man
call a woman
cunt
gives me the same
feeling
as hearing a
white person
call
a black person
nigger
and he's kind of
nodding
kind of
nervous
saying sorry
sorry
if i offended you
she was a cunt,
though.

## MR. BUZZLE

mr. buzzle, please don't be dead,
never even got to dedicate my first novel to you.
teaching catholic school must have worked your nerves,
preaching from the closet about hell and crucifixion
when all you wanted to do was direct an 8th grade
production of *cats* or *phantom of the opera* bossing us
around in your beret and long cigarettes like some
new york city hotshot, mr. buzzle, please don't be dead,
i never even got to name my first child after you.
remember when the principal made me cry on graduation day,
saying my sleeveless dress was immoral and cheap
and you called her a bitch, you had nothing to lose,
she had already fired you for being queer and calling
your students *mary sunshine* and spending too much time
on art, mr. buzzle, please don't be dead i know,
they think all fags have aids
and you're sitting in a piano bar
somewhere singing show tunes
you're vacationing in provincetown with your
culture vulture boyfriend you're receiving
a glorious blow job in sister gertrude's honor,
remember how tight her sweaters were and
she never wore her veil, remember she'd
charge into class after prayer and pull me
into the bathroom to scrub off all my eyeliner
she was so sure i was going to end up pregnant
but you knew better, didn't you mr. buzzle,
please don't be dead.

## LOVESAD

i want to
sit in a bar, dark,
with poets drinking beer.
lovesad'll do that it
gets you up gets you movin' i
haven't written a word in
six weeks and now my
brain's reeling in fat ones they're
written before i can pick up
a pen puts you on a bus like
sending you off to camp and
you wake up in arizona makes you
feel righteous drinking liquor in
a room with no one else like my momma
always warned first sign of an
alcoholic got you poppin' chocolate too,
you need it, some lovestarved hormone
it's replacing, this is science.
lovesad's got you nervous changes
coffee to blood makes you jesus
lovesad's got you singing
smiths songs got you feeling
ghost lips on your neck got you
tugging at your hair like it's
hiding all the answers makes you
hate all your friends for being
nice to you it's twisting all
your insides welding
smoke chains to your lips
making sleep a precious fossil and
three times as rare.

# GAZPACHO

1:30 a.m. gazpacho in my room
red and green and tasting
like tucson like too much
parsley and cocktails on
the porch, mezcal, tastes
like tequila someone played
a trick on we bought it cheap
in mexico two bottles per gringo
over the border gazpacho and
burritos enough to feed the
neighborhood and i did because
the neighborhood was crashing
at my house showing up at sunset
to eat at my cinderblock table but
it was cool i could afford it could
afford to pay rent buy groceries buy
jugs of red wine to get them all drunk
bongs of pot to keep them stoned and
gas tank full for road trips i
was making lots of cash and we were all
cool liberal fuck liberal we were
radical, anarchist cookbook beside
the moosewood cookbook on our bookshelf we
knew all about things like the
distribution of wealth and like i said i
was making tons of money and they weren't
making any they were unemployed because
finding work is hard or they're students or
in the emergency stage of the sexual abuse thing or
some other piece of laziness doctored up as
politics you know capitalism blah blah blah so
i was supporting an ever-changing band of lethargic
sunbathing potheads because i was making so much
money and yeah i was making it by leaving my body
so that strange men could fill it like a kind of
demon spirit but fuck it was my choice no gun
to my head no linda lovelace scene here and
i was really into communal living and we were all

such free spirits, crossing the country we were
nomads and artists and no one ever stopped
to think about how the one working class housemate
was whoring to support a gang of upper middle class
deadheads with trust fund safety nets and connecticut
childhoods, everyone was too busy processing their
isms to deal with non-issues like class
and besides,
you don't think rich families have problems
you don't think rich families have secret rapes and
alcoholic dads and feed their kids bad food with
sugar and preservatives i mean when you
get right down to it we're all just humans,
all on the same path to destruction because
our mother earth is being raped (is it ok
if we borrow that term from your
oppression, it's really powerful) anyway,
that class trip is just divide and conquer,
blood money is just a redundant phrase and all work
is prostitution, right? and it's so cool
how none of them have hang-ups about
sex work they're all real
open-minded real
revolutionary you know
the legal definition of pimp is
one who lives off the earnings of
a prostitute, one or five or
eight and i'd love to stay and
eat some of the stir fry i've been cooking
for y'all but i've got to go fuck
this guy so we can all get stoned and
go for smoothies tomorrow, save me
some rice, ok?

## SUSHI

and this town is too small
to be writing poetry about
one night stands
it's like that sushi bar where
the sushi floats around in front of you
on little wooden boats
if you just sit there
puckering your tongue with
pickled ginger
the one you want
eventually floats by
and she is like sushi because
she seems raw and because
you don't eat sushi,
because it makes you think
of some perfect fish
getting its scales torn off or
twisting crazy trying to find
some moisture in the air,
to breathe;
and she makes you think
of some perfect little girl
getting her skin pushed in
until her brain flops
right out of her body
and sushi looks so pretty,
it doesn't even look dead it looks
like jewelry;
she wears her deaths well, too,
she is hung with them like
ornaments
and you have words to say
about violence and abuse,
let them well in your throat
like a drunk's last sleep
when she is spread over you like cream
it is not the time to tell her
exactly what you think

about sex involving weaponry
how the knife she trails
down your body
makes your cunt
feel like butter
how dairy products
hide their death so well.

## OF COURSE

and of course i
couldn't write a poem
about her until
she made me cry, not
one about her cleaning
my room shoving all my body's
dirty colors into the closet so
i'm searching for my socks on hands
and knees and washing all my
teacups growing lily pads of
mold and crusted bowls of soup and
how she translated lyrics in french
for me so i wouldn't feel left out when
everyone was singing and
i tried to once it was going to
say something sappy like teach me
to write a love poem that isn't full
of salt and pain but it didn't work,
some poet gene predisposed to only
find inspiration in hurt and
of course there's no place in
my house to smoke heartbreak
cigarettes that sneezing roommate
allergic to incense cats and
people i could sit outside
in the driveway with the
junkies she's always trying to
call the cops on or fumigate
my bedroom with the window
open polluting the hummingbird's
bottle brush dinner i could
take a walk or sit inside and
sulk and cry and celebrate
the consolation prize of a
momentary lapse of writer's
block before it gets stuffed like
my red and squeaking nose there
are feelings so big they can only

be written on skin there
are lungs that seize with toxic
tornadoes and the pain
of tattooing your heart
to your body
doesn't ever relieve
the one inside.

# THE CITY AT THE END OF THE WORLD

pure tragedy press
1997

# A GOOD THING TO SAY

to a girl dying by the hour
as the meter ticks on the van
and the money machine shits cash
into the palms of the lucky
as i screech a rake through the days
and revise every approach,
tilt angles into graphs and cubes
that send me sprawling dizzy
in the sun waiting for another
call so i can run naked into the street
and really start to hate you for everything
you don't allow to happen, here where
the traffic lights are and the cops and
the wires strung above the roofs like
our city's been netted and they're just
waiting for us all to dry up and die
and we are, and i offer up water
the most of my body, sweat and piss
and spit and you wipe your mouth
and turn, your feet on the cracking street.

## I'M GETTING REALLY SICK OF
## WRITING POEMS LIKE THIS

either way it's awful,
either you have no curiosity, simply
don't care or you have this terrible,
gleeful restraint, a will turned in on itself.
it's the closest i can come to understanding
sin, this turning away from living or something,
like clean your plate
somewhere people are starving somewhere
people are desperate somewhere
people are only around for a minute and
your clock is ticking as you dump me at the
nightly curb and go away again.
i climb the nightly stairs, tug off
my boots, sit down at my window
and cry. it's my new job, it's gross
it's so routine, the nightly cry above the streets,
my landscape, the row of darkly gleaming cars
parked against the margin, the drunk boys next door
out all night with their bottles and their radio,
they've got this great radio that looks like the grill
of a caddy, you'd like it, you, you, you,
you're like the invisible pet on a stiff leash
that i walk through the day, a joke,
and it was almost funny
when that girl asked
if we were together
i really didn't know what to say
i really didn't know we were on a date
i feel like i've got this really great girlfriend
who won't kiss me, i know all these
things, like to get you
two hash browns at McDonald's
because you like to tuck one
beneath the bun of your
sausage McMuffin, stupid shit
that makes me feel more important
than i am, like the manager at Walgreen's

gave me a little badge and i get to be his
assistant, glorified cashier, this is dumb
these metaphors are awful, i'm horribly,
terribly in love with you, and you love it or
it makes you nervous.

the heat has burned our houses down
people are rushing into traffic clutching
gigantic bottles of beer, desperately trying
to live up to the beauty in the air,
the gorgeous smell of it, it stinks like a carnival;
like big adventure,
like something you've never seen
is right around the corner
and everyone is insane,
plunging bare-chested into traffic
to find it,
at the edge of the corner
waiting for it to pull up in a caddy
while i get dropped off at the curb.
 you're like the best swimming pool
with the slide and the diving board
in the backyard of the neighbor who hates you
you sit on the porch all summer
watching them swim.
this would be a really great time to leave town.
this would be a really fabulous time
to hop a terrible bus
and be gone.
the sun will be back around tomorrow,
bully-brutal, and i will walk into the giant lie
of the day with you laughing till it sinks.

## PERCENTAGES

i can't even try to get past
a sky like this one.
like a duck or a kid in a
plastic rain jacket i move
through morning.
it sucks that everyone is up,
people should sleep more,
wake easy like a tide that carries you
to the shore of your bed,
no alarms to scare your dreams away.
once i was always awake
in the cold damp morning,
with coffee and a greasy croissant
i thought i had to work the whole day,
i was so scared of falling into
prostitution.
so i sat at a computer
and then at a desk.
every day,
little snack in between.
hateful coworkers.
now i sleep til ten
but not today
today i'm part of the special club,
privy to the secrets of eight a.m.
mission rain
*good morning*
says my curbside grocer
*need anything*
oh yes oh i do oh if only,
if only, a long thin needle
to plunge into my heart's
sore muscle oh it just has been
beating forever, pop it
like a wet balloon,
lay me back on my bed
this horrible morning
i hunt bagels like

small animals, sometimes
i feel so primitive, my teeth,
illogical hair between my legs,
claws at the tip of my fingers
that's why i like to sniff
your head, roll you over
and jump on your back.
here i am in the wet
and rainy jungle with all
the other animals, the big sad
ocean of humanity
making us soar above bowls
of frothy coffee,
drafty tables.
sometimes i love myself so much
i shake with it, an extension
of the street's gorgeous garbage
sometimes i miss people i
don't know so much i cry
in my french fries,
my sweet sweet juice.
i am so sad today,
i am beautiful with it
really feeling my heart
the real thing the muscular one,
not the vague poetic heart
or even the common dull ache.
a true quick turning as it
raised its strong back
like a whale in the sea and
spit steam for just a second.
and then i was just a regular body,
wet-eyed and tortured by
a brush with something beautiful.
i want to ride in this sadness
like a car that takes me deeper
into the place i live, more green
and sun, round things
like hills.
i will sit in the back

in a cool pair of shades,
flicking my ashes in an empty
can of coke, strung out,
leaning my head into
the loud loud radio
feeling great, crying behind
my dark plastic eyes.
it's that active kind of sadness
that moves me through the outdoors
where the sun has finally arrived
but too late the morning sky
has strained my back.
today i am learning about learning,
in a room with all these nonprofit people,
stream people aids people
runaway homeless youth people.
i am the tree people
woodland creature people
i hold the elevator door
so it doesn't snap
on all the different people.
like holden caulfield
i want to stand here forever,
leaning on the jerking jaws.
so, do you want to know
how adults learn.
1% is smell, that's
the animal part, picking up
the subtlest most ancient waves
like invisible strings that tug
at your brain,
my nose in your hair.
1.5% is touch,
now that's hard to believe
the whole landscape of skin
hardly worth more than a nose.
oh but i've made a mistake-
1% of learning is taste
not smell
smell is a whopping 3.5%

edged out by hearing with 11%
and because the eyes are the most
ambitious part of the brain,
tunneling out into the world like
watery slugs nesting in bone
humans learn 85% by sight.
if you add all this up it equals
i don't really know you at all
yet here you are
oh the drama oh the pain
oh the slow drags of the cigarette
some cigarettes let you know
they're killing you, how they
rake your throat
and leave you stinking
but some are more about
their hot and burning tip,
a slow smolder you can eat.
when humans learn through a blend
of telling and showing
they can recall 65%
three days later.
i made a friend
she went away
and already i've lost
35% of who she was.
like the smoke on my cigarette,
into the air and gone.

## LAURIE

i feel i must write
a poem
for laurie
who finds deja
vu comforting
cause it makes her think
she's supposed to be
here, lounging
with her hangover
telling us
about being a baby
looking tightly
at everyone's
faces.
that is unusual,
for someone so small
to have
such focus.
it's easy
to imagine laurie
as a baby
because her head
is so naked & new.

i must interrupt
this poem
to talk about
the flea that just leapt
from o i don't
want to think about
where the flea leapt from
but it landed
on this page
here on the bus.
this is the 2nd
bus ride
i took
with a flea.

they are my
new pets,
sleeping under my covers
like cats
but not so cozy
& harder to cuddle.
i hate them.
they will be exterminated
and the landlord will have to pay
because we, his poor tenants,
are broke.

back to laurie
and the perfect stripe
of hair
rolled on her head
like a pastry.
laurie's new glasses
make her look
like a spaceship
something strong
with metal wings.
they're her
special glasses,
not for
everyday use.

when i cry
in my garlic
laurie's eyes move back
deeper
and i peek
at her mysterious
places.
don't we all have
a place
that never stops crying.
now i can feel
like part of a larger
movement of misery

rather than trapped
in the busted elevator
of my heart.
laurie ushered me into
my archetypal experience
over potatoes and coffee.
it was easier
than cigarettes
and the way they
rough up your lungs.
now i am an initiate
of some unspoken order,
my reformed heart
in its tangle of veins
rationing beats
to the rest of my body
with the calm
generosity
of one rich enough
to spare it.
time to go.
like the deer
in the nature video
i'm watching at work
i will bounce
my spotted body
into the gorgeous
who knows.

## NATURE VIDEO

it is sad
that the old rock
bridge will snap and
shatter into the stream
that made it.
beautiful and destined
to collapse, nature
is ruthless.
pay your respect
to the crumbled bridge
on the discovery channel
and put some pants
on the antelope
that bull's-eye of fur
around their ass
is obscene.
the antelope
are sexy animals
parading
their blatant behinds
for the tourists.
and what about
the anasazi
the narrator tells me
they're gone
where
did they go
anasazi
means ancient.
in tucson
i ate ancient
anasazi beans
in my delicious
green pasta.
they left
these homes
they built
back when people

moved like glaciers
or wind.
ok
here is the scoop
on the anasazi:
ana means
enemy
not ancient
and they used up all
their water
and split
leaving us these
honeycomb houses
like prehistoric
playgrounds
to climb upon
and videotape.

what else about
nature
it's nice,
kind of
supernatural, really
like when i think
other planets,
take mars,
i think of
the grand canyon.
i spent a moment
on the edge
of the tallest rock
and realized vertigo
isn't fear
it's the desire
to ball your life up
in your fist
and plummet
so incredibly high
and no fences
where are the people

who put up all the fences
and the orange stickers
and the safety belts
how did this
enormous rock
slip past them.
no one tells me
to leave
as i stand
so close
to my most glorious
death, here
in ruthless
nature.
i laid on my back
arms splayed like
a kid in a snowdrift.
i laid there.
it was all
i could do
in the face
of this impossible
planet.

## THE CITY AT THE END OF THE WORLD

I Was Still Drunk
When I Woke Up, she
was saying to me, How
Did That Happen?
count, two in the house
one down the street
when i felt every voice on the planet
begging me to smash it.
who doesn't love the sound
of something crashing,
a car down the block, out of sight,
the sound of helpless tires
desperate clutching the pavement
i didn't smash the bottle.
i left it on the trash can
out front of the bar
and inside the bar i drank water,
played pinball, waited for my life to happen.
one cautious beer in the next bar
and then one reckless one
when she went away in her car
and i sat on the bathroom floor like
a crumpled paper towel that didn't make it
to the basket. i played a song on the jukebox.
i played it again. i played it again.
i played it three times, i gave the thing
my dollar and it only
played it once. one friend got up
and played it one more time,
another ran to the store
to buy me cigarettes
and girls i didn't know dropped
Camels into my lap, everyone
felt bad for me
sobbing at the bar
in my reckless beer.
what could be worse than the sober bartender
who goes to AA meetings with my ex-girlfriend

and the other girl who stays away from me
because i drink too much and my life
is a mess and i'm out of control,
mopping up my crying with a sponge.
You're Like A Vegan Working At McDonald's
i told her
but what better place for a christian
than in a den of sinners.
one more beer at home, a can
from the fridge at the computer
typing out the history
of all my hope and sadness,
tossing it into your life
with the push of a button.
it was like the button that starts the end
of the world, all the dread and evil
of a single button, like the urge to kick
a puppy when nobody's looking.
i pushed the button. i blew everything up.
i went to bed, woke up,
didn't know where i was.
in my roommate's room all the morning flies
were buzzing in the air, and the floor
was a mess of power tools, skateboards,
clothes and ashtrays. i sat up in bed
and i could have been anywhere
someplace hot where the air never moves,
with a sun like a mean dad burning in the sky
everyone tiptoeing under his glare
the city at the end of the world where everyone's given up
sitting on the orange pavement
drowsy in the weather
something wet in your hand to drink, it's where i live.
i walk into my room and everything is regular.
i take a shower i put clothes on
i dry my hair i blow the fuse
i did it. i blew it up again.

## IMPOSSIBLE

today was the longest day,
held me frozen in its slowness.
sitting where she sat
on the flat comer of my bed
just watching the day fall grey
outside my filthy windows,
the grime on the floor,
thick dust in the corners,
you'd think nobody lived here.
creatures creating themselves
in bottles, musty clothes and
the phone doesn't ring.
i'm not sad, the day is,
watch it sobbing in the street
and me at my wet window,
rapunzel.

i marked the spot where she sat,
unthinking, fuzzy pink pen
in my absent hand.
i was waiting for years and
today the waiting was sharpest
and i suppose i'll be waiting forever,
trying to see my room, bright & dirty,
through eyes she kept closed.

i thought that i liked girls
who really are boys but
i learned that really
the girls i like are dogs,
the shaggy wet one that rolled
on my bed, impossible
my arms up her shirt
pressing skin feeling the hard
dark place the words come from.
it just all feels forever different, life,
but why should it, taking my impossible
heart. on the bus, this boy i sort of know

climbed on, he's kind of like
jimi hendrix or a gypsy with a
beaded face, glittered eyes
stoned i bet and i guess
the world will expect me to
go on talking, paying bills,
the rumbling bus that pulled me to work,
you know when you have to pretend
to be sick so eventually you are or
maybe i am sick truly sick with
impossible waiting.
why didn't you call me?
my little code scratched on
the paper you jammed in your pocket,
lost ignored maybe soaked with the rain
that drummed down on our heads
as we ran to the drugstore to buy
you tampons, my favorite impossible,
you leaving puddles in the most mundane
aisle of my life, pulling a blue box
from the shelf in the angry glare of
walgreens where nobody knows it
is you, the shaggy prince of everything
the woman who took your money,
ladies buying christmas appliances and
i really can't believe it, with you
in this torn little corner of my life.
i wanted to ask you if you enjoyed
the storm, tell you how it ate houses
smashed trees blew in glass hurt
a lot of people but i hardly noticed it,
somewhere in the safe bright
of my messy room i was the storm,
the way it shakes the place out
like looking for lost keys
or a woman on a plane, gone.

did i not kiss you correctly?
pushing my wet leg to yours
time bright as the bulb on my ceiling

i wanted everything, wanted
to eat that moment, all its teeth
and lips, listen to the stupid thing
you didn't say find the hair
that got lost in my mouth
feed you my fingers, make the waiting
go backwards i am queen of it now,
bride of impossible moments,
everything pulled inside out and
solid so now at my window
you are here, this,
a woman i will write
poems to, not something
that hung in my air no more
something outside
that felt like in.
the wet impossible poet,
like a dog she
pressed her head to my chest
i know because i was there
does that count
the warm cup on my floor
the fruity smell she didn't swallow.
it wasn't her on the phone,
it was some guy asking me to read
pornographic poetry
at a performance
but i don't write like that,
my writing is waiting for something
that already happened,
pulling it back, over
and over, impossible.

# THE ARMAGEDDON DANCE

the guy tore into his scratcher
at my special table.
there was all this gummy dust
and the useless loser ticket and
then he left and i could sit down.
i guess it's a lucky day
for no one but me.
a little fame, a little
glory, a little voice
at the end of the line
saying *what,*
*tell me all about it.*
i know the nasty things
she wants to hear, that one.
she's lying in her bed,
she's really just so striking
and i'm at my job in the office
twitching in the chair
with the little wheels
and on the wall are pictures,
oscar wilde, patti smith,
some friends, devils
aliens and a pink post-it:
I'm So Bad At Seduction
It's Really Pathetic.
kind of an affirmation,
i thought it would make
a good poem, better poem
than moment
aren't all the poems
a salvaged piece
of something awful.
take it churn it burn
it make me a hero
for a minute for just
a second.
i am so lucky
to have this girl

on the phone, wanting
my voice. i call
airlines, i write
poems for her
she makes big and
secret plans, i smell them
like a fat cake baking,
i drool. she goes
through the city
looking for me
and the point is not
to find me.
i'm a work in progress
a conceptual dance
called armageddon
and what if
nobody gets it
or what if she doesn't know
how to do it right
it doesn't matter,
it simply has to be done,
it was too late
the moment it started,
we were locked into the ride
and the car began to climb.
isn't it exciting
i love the way i smell
after i've been with you
the stink of your hair
on my hands, greasy,
and the endless cigarettes
we have our songs and
our smells and the deep
red landscape of the
front seat, the people
of the 2 am streets
witness to me losing it all
beneath your teeth
and fingers, the stumbling
drunk glance through your

spotted window i
am too lucky to care
o find me find me come
and get me and
i know you will.

## PIGEONS

you know, everybody in this neighborhood
smokes. it's a good place for me to be
my pack tucked into the pocket
of my new blue sweatshirt with the hood,
i'm gonna trick it out, patches, chunks
of metal but right it's just this
warm rag. o i am never short on vision,
the skateboard that rolls me through this place.
i blend in here so neatly in my shabby sweatshirt
at the special table, round plastic on the street
outside the grocery store where daily
the desperate smokers stare at the sidewalk
and breathe. o i really do belong here,
it's really too perfect
like the drunken trudge to the arco
at 3 am for the 3rd pack of cigarettes
that i kept leaving behind, losing at bars
forgetting in cars, my boots hit the pavement
so hard and it was like my insides had grown
to form a city and i paved a street and walked it.
packs of drunk men, come on fuck with me
fuck with me i've got boots on need cigarettes
drank too much am desperate am in love
am daring something big to crack me open
and let me prove for once that i really am
the queen of this. my bulletproof smokes
and a jar of juice that was disgusting.
i did not need the last beer,
it's like you unhinged a jaw in me
a fleshy tide pulling the worst of the world
in through my window, pay phone on the corner
ringing all night long
if i can't have you then i want everything else
the poems of every desperate loser
who knew this insane gravity,
the rise and fall of you inside me
like a terrible life half-lived.
the skin around your eyes,

your gas station of hair,
it's just not enough
the grope in the seat of after-school specials,
your runaway loves your secret revolutions
my puke in the toilet at 4 am
it's so beautiful and it's just not enough
what could you give me to plug it all up.
am i supposed to calm down now?
i'm giving all my cigarettes away
to the neighborhood, flinging them from trains
like eva peron, waving my poems at the poor.
we need to smoke, there is little else to do
in the face of all this, the whistling hooker
on the corner, old man leaning
into the oxygen tank, tugging it behind him
like a sick and willful dog.
shopping cart of rusting flowers.
there's an artist in the darkest apartment
on the very next block
and you'll never see his paintings.
they're beautiful.
he sits in the dark
surrounded by pictures of black women
nursing white babies, black men
with rope around their necks, malcolm x
and on the television jane seymour says
Anxiety? Thinking About Your Waist Size
After Having Two Kids, That's Anxiety.
i guess the rest of us are experiencing
something different out here on the sidewalk.
i guess we'll have to invent a new word
for all this. what should it sound like.
something too thick for the tongue to form.
something guttural like a burp,
the tongue tastes it as it talks,
something that sounds like love.
the pigeons of this city have been making
me sick. a team of them attacking
a leathery chunk of chicken in the gutter,
it's cannibalism. then a dead one, plump

and solid at the bus stop just like a real animal.
i think my love is a pigeon,
part of the urban landscape.
they used to be called rock doves
until there were just so many of them,
how could we call them doves.
a grey word for their overcast bodies.
i'm glad somebody saw me writing this.
it's like nothing exists unless i tear off its clothes
and kick it naked into the streets.
everyone kept asking Did She
Touch Your Boob Did She
Touch Your Boob, it's this little joke
and then you did and then i
had to tell them and immediately
i felt so dumb, like it's all just a cigarette
to flick out your window as we cruise
the apocalypse. but the world already ended,
back when we were teenagers.
what is this fake place we occupy,
digging our paws into the pavement,
trying to get something back,
my love a time capsule
stuffed with tv guides and old notebooks,
my love a bruised pigeon
flying into a plate glass sky.

## MY PLACE IN THE WORLD

the heat of the streets
doesn't quite reach me
it laps at the curbs like
a glaring tide, seeming soft
though really it's a killer.
the bums inside this place
talking all day about
panama, vietnam and
tijuana. and always
the women, stacked
like beer in the fridge,
icy.
or else the melting racks
of chocolate. i wonder
if the woman behind the counter
wants to kill them.
all night i dreamt
of killing men.
he was a real
bastard, grimy hat
and ancient face,
something sunning itself forever
on the brutal streets that curiously
does not die. i beat him
with a bat. it felt good.
now that everything
has calmed down a little
i can dream again,
it was just too much
drama for a little while,
too much theater and my
nights were filled
with dark nothing.
now i kill men.
i knew it would come to this.
flying in a big airplane
reading that awful book,
*Mercy* and the moral

of the story is start
killing bums. the men
of the street. work
your way up
to the other ones.
it seemed to make sense
everything else only
gets you in the papers,
a quick blab before the camera.
so these men, i sit here
with them now, all of us
smoking and it seems
i have found a legion
of grandfathers.
i like the idea
of a disconnected people
connected in a strange
dense way like cables
beneath the ground.
i don't want to kill them.
it's like signing onto
a major label, right?
an angry girl
frozen in the sky
stares down on me
with kill in her eyes.
everywhere i belong
and the places i do not
it's just a thicker tangle
of cable, harder
to place.

## LAST HOPE

stop with that cigarette blowing its ashes in my coffee.
chocolate crumbs are ok so the red plastic ashtray
goes under the table, but everyone can eat my brownie.
talk about teeth. sini's got twelve bad ones,
at $800 a tooth. we all get quiet and do the math,
think about that for a minute.

there's nothing to be done about a cigarette smoked,
about big feelings melted into puddles,
flooding out from a tent somewhere in michigan.
don't talk to me about it two years later
in a bar when i have never slept.

everyone heard my secrets tonight
and each time it rang like a lie.
please don't tell me to take her in the bathroom
and fuck her. can i have a cigarette?
i'm trying to quit, that's why i don't have
any. really, i'm really trying to quit.
everything. my look is all wrong.
i'm so quiet inside but i'm a circus elephant
entering the room, a parade of jerks,
a rain of frogs, in love like an idiot girl
with a song she wrote inside her head.

i'd really like to buy the world a coke.
one coke for everyone and be done with it.
then i could really relax. o come into
my arms love let me crawl up your history,
press myself against you
like dead flowers on the page.

i brush my teeth just like the lady showed me.
my brush angled, the sharp rub of the floss,
it takes forever. like meditation, water falling
foam frothing from my lips into the molding sink.
life is rampant in my home and it is gross.
i'm sick of everyone. except her. she's my last hope,

religion or the snack you stashed for yourself
at the back of the fridge. i almost forgot i had it.
there, behind the pickles. it's you.

# THE BIGGEST MISTAKE I MADE ALL YEAR

so i thought i'd see how many girls
i could engage and detach
in an admirably short period of time,
how many heads could be cut
on the block of my bed, casualties
of the casual, bleeding like that boy
on the pissy street, remember, the
two o'clock shots that startled you
as i released the blade and ruined
my futon. isn't it a shock
when the sirens suddenly stop
and the blue lights thump against
your windows.
you forgot they had
a purpose.
let's say that a house is a body
and these windows the ribs where i sit,
pumping smoke. in a minute
a woman will arrive with a camera
to shoot my antisocial vagina.
she loves to have her picture taken,
but if you touch her she'll puke.
like a terrible baby she cries,
red-faced,
till i take her to my bed
and burp her on my shoulder.
and who decided we can smoke
all over the house.
who was in charge of deciding that.
why is there a giant ashtray in the shower,
the most sacred room, a chapel really
a temple with its many ointments and
naked chambers. i lather my pussy
and perm her hair, brush her curls,
suck from a two-liter bottle of coke
at my window, dripping ashes on the children
who skate around the parking meter,
imagine if water was living,

how gross we'd all feel climbing out
of the shower. but it is living, right,
everything is living and doubtlessly
i am here for a reason.
i wish i had something to tell you,
something new, something you have never
heard before. maybe you are more complex.
than me, everyone. smoking on your steps
beside the pale buddha that stares
at the wall, the buddha thing to do.
as long as i don't love you i can do this for you,
a vigil at the sooty window
with a two-liter bottle of coke.
it's like church. you can have one
or the other
but you can't have both.
did you know we're in outer space?
i always forget. missing the trees
for the forest, the candy for the garland
of gum wrappers, evolution
for the garbage that's making my block
look so ugly. and i am complex,
in a simple way. i can't find my heart
but something is keeping me going.
my room is a mess, i've yet to leave you
at the curb for the monday morning men.
but you're not even here! just like god.
you're catholic, right, so you know what it is
to talk to empty presence. you know
what it's like to be stuck in a myth at birth.
when i was a girl i thought i'd be a saint.
i thought i'd be the vessel for the second coming
and i do believe that is what happened
you know what my favorite vice is.
right now there is a child in my house
and what will they give her to suck on,
faith tits a piece of plastic.
this could go on forever
if i don't put an end to it
and isn't that always
the problem

## OUR LADY OF RIDICULOUS WISHES

i don't want to pray to madonna, i
want to pray to whoever madonna prayed to
to get every little girl thing she wanted.
queen of the little girls now madonna tries
to be a grown-up but we all see right through her.
i want to pray to whoever gave madonna
all the things she ever prayed for that
everyone knows she has.
it would be stupid to pray to madonna.
she's not even dead.
she could be the saint of something important
in our world but she has to prove herself first
with the dying. and i could pray to her,
grinding my knees into the floorboards
splintering my knees on blue paint chips,
the fat bodies of flies upended at the
bottom of my room. dirtying my knees on
bits of eyeliner, on different cosmetics
would be the way to pray to madonna who
has maybe gotten everything she wanted.
it is true you have, got to know the right people,
even as you tuck yourself into bed and
fold your hands beneath the pillow.
my city is brighter when you are here because
like god or madonna you could be anywhere.
i could see you in the street, in line for a burrito
we could share a seat on the bus it really
drives home certain buddhist thoughts like
the possibilities of emptiness.
matter being born into space, a prince
bursting from the gang of everyday
that clogs my sidewalks.
i want to carry your head like a purse,
braid your hair into straps that swing
from my hand as i sleuth
through the city.
open the clasp of your skull to poke around
at everything i have ever wanted.

and i am
i want like a lion,
it's what causes the most suffering, desire,
and waiting, and time which of course
does not exist. then what am i doing
between now and every wish i have
coming true. there's no art in this.
it stumbles out of me, tripping down the street
after you, bumbling and gangly like
a little girl who doesn't believe in god.
like the unholiness of being twelve.
a girl twitches in bed on christmas eve,
wracked with the promise of morning
and if christmas never came
would it prolong the excitement
or would she just grow up.
are you there: madonna?
it's me, michelle.

## NICE TRY

she sees me big
as a blimp in her vision
bright as a bright idea
big as a revolution
of barefoot children
big as a drag queen
so i buy boas.

i buy two.

in the store the drag queens go to
a wall of feathers, marked by price
according to the hierarchy of bird
they came from.

i take chicken.
i take two.

i paint my toes
to match my fingers
as they poke out the mouth
of my mules.
i tie on a swish of cloth
pluck my legs hair
by hair
keeping me awake for days.
i color my hair i color my eyes
i color the sky i color everything
i fall
down the stairs
with my suitcase
when she comes.
she is sleek and easy
inside the morning
and i have chicken feathers
frothing at my throat.
this is a dumb magic
the deities who watch over

behavior like this
are deceitful,
i don't trust them.
she carries my suitcase
i walk good in those shoes
the pavement has more to fear
than i do.
in the airport everyone looks
but they'd do that anyway
they think she's a boy and i'm crazy.
the detector detects metal
at her back
*it's my bra* she says
and he turns all red,
Sorry.

in the car with the top down
the boa flips like a thing still living
spitting feathers at the freeway
we leave it like road kill. we drive,
we drive on and on, we drive
forever we drive three hours
looking for a taco bell
in la as the sun
smacks our heads
like good sense.
there are no taco bells
in la, there is everything
but taco bells
and hustlers.
i am in dumb shoes
that work my skin
to blister, i am in
hollywood
and the hustlers are gone
i am hungry wrapped in feathers
in love with a pair of eyes fixed
to the road i need mexican pizza
side of guacamole side of sour cream
ice tea steak taco veggie fajita i need

a shallow history of heartache
to fling myself into i need
the back wheels to catch this costume
like isadora, snap me back
from the ghosts of catty tragedies
that line the empty streets
of this place.

## THE BIG ONE'S NOT COMING

the one the rest of the country's been waiting for,
patiently impatient for the bad teenager to overdose,
slide from the earth into myth,
my rickety porch a pile of garbage
it's not going to happen.

it's not going to happen,
armaggedon, fire erupting
from the flat streets of my life,
silver ships filling the sky like rain
children, old men rushing into the outside
with guns bullets like more rain
cracking my flat streets the fall
of civilization,
all dogs turning on their masters
and taking the flat streets
a bubble of love
popping in your brain
like an aneurysm
and you come in your car
in the throes of a gorgeous death

it's not going to happen,
a plummet from the endless window
television static at the end of the night
it's not going to happen
the corpse of every bitter life
dragging their ass from the dirt
to say everything that died in their mouth
as their last breath wheezed

it's not going to happen
the big one's not coming
peace, respite, a gleaming gold dad
from the sky, all the parents in the world
looking up in united comprehension, finally,
as their children drop dead from exhaustion
your love storming the jungle in a ski hat

kicking lead from the wall as it climbs my hair
it's not going to happen
i've got the flat streets a landscape to share with the planet
flat and filthy and nobody is coming
to clean it, it's not going to happen
and it's all we've got forever

## WHAT I MEAN BY AMERICAN

i don't know what to tell you
when you're just so close,
hanging in front of me
like a wondrous new planet
no one knows the name of.
the orbit
is truly dizzying.
when you leave i can sit
with my feet on my window
and pretend i have a brain
that thinks truly wondrous thoughts
when like a toy it only clicks
you you you, truly wondrous,
each letter a chunk of crystal sugar
on the back of a candy worm,
the gunfire crack of a backfiring car,
some great explosion leaving ash
like burnt sugar, you know, sticky
the way sugar turns
when you clutch it in your palm
fingers in a sweet fist my thoughts of you
coins falling from the luckiest slot
in las vegas, someplace neither of us
have been, someplace we're bound for.
i want to move deeper into you
like a chugging bus that pulls me into
america, her gas stations and empty
diners, the rusting metal insects
sipping delicately from the earth
as the sun falls down and bangs its
head and i charge fully-armed
into your heart and hold up
your convenience store.
something like that,
something truly american.
i'm sick of living on the outskirts
of this country.
i want to immerse myself

in all its dust and terror
i want you in the getaway car
as i charge through the parking lot
dripping cheetos and iced sugar and
thin green bills to feed us.
i build a country
and take you on vacation
build parents
for you to run away from
put some clouds in the sky
the way you like
build a car from the ground up
rust on my hands
leave the keys in the ignition
and wait for you to steal it.

## PICKUP TRUCKS

maybe the most beautiful moment ever
was pulling out of the desert propped up
in the back of a pickup truck, watching
the sky collapse into a purple-orange mess,
watching it all get pulled away, the dusky lumps
of hill, rocks that stopped mid-crumble,
silhouettes of sad cactus, it was like a strong
and noble lover who didn't want you
if you were stupid enough to leave.
the whole scene was like a postcard
or a painting, too gorgeous to be something
you could walk into the middle of,
you doubted its existence even as you
watched it, so enormous and incredible
and proud like it knew its only job
was to just be there, that perfect.

tonight i rumbled on my back,
flat in another pickup truck,
getting that weird view of this city,
the endless wires that hook the whole place
together, the frosted tops of our corroding
birthday cake homes, they're beautiful,
chunks of whipped cream topping
hardening to scabs and flaking into the streets.
just because something is beautiful
doesn't mean it will be cared for
is no guarantee it's even wanted

i sucked down an oyster at a barbecue
more sport than eating
it lodged than passed through my throat
like a fleshy pill trailing horseradish.
i ate chicken and grilled salmon and
chunks of potato salad with my fingers
i hadn't eaten all day so it was really great
to arrive at such a feast
and all my friends were impressed

that i had brought them to the home
of people who ate so good.
the next party was raver stoner all-boy
fiesta, maybe 3 girls, so straight
it was like wild kingdom, watching them.
you brought me watermelon, thank you,

at the bar, you thought of me today
when i wasn't there to poke you
with my presence, but i didn't write
on the bathroom wall for you
and you wrote nothing for me
and obviously something's amiss,
the wrong forces are at work here

i really hate wanting something like this
i'm like all the girls who didn't make the squad
this season, i'm picking up all kinds of
secondary habits to pull me through this
shitty night. if i got whacked by a car
just think of the desert of cactus
that would bloom in your guts.
it's all i imagine.
i am so careful walking through the world,
moving with caution so i can live long enough
to give you another chance.

## COPS

at the wells fargo bank machines
the multicultural mission district
police force
is bothering this tattooed guy
beaten-looking like a ratty old chair.
there's a white guy cop, asian guy
cop dyke cop
patting down
his sour levis
they want to look inside
his velcro wristband,
beneath his baseball hat
would probably love
to get their fingers up his ass.
does the dyke cop
try extra hard
or is she really like that
mirrored sunglasses
and that bad lesbian
police officer hairdo.

do the police know now
that everyone hates them
what do we have to do
to really drive it home
like the baton on my chest
at that protest.
watch them
walking around,
doing this incredibly noble job
that everyone wishes
they'd stop doing.
you'd think they'd feel silly,
especially all dressed up
in those costumes.

if i stare too long
at the cop

can he arrest me
like the italian girls
at the roller rink
when i was 13
*gotta starin' problem*
i am mesmerized
by thick black belts
slung heavy on their waists
the stiff guns, little pockets of mace
walkie talkie and that smooth
length of nightstick
i know a few girls that gear
would look great on
a few hands that could pull
weaponry from their waist
and really do something to me.
if you're a dyke
it helps to be comfortable
with paradoxes like these.

i'm always searching
for the cop that stole my poetry
at a demonstration.
i chucked it at his head
they said it was evidence,
i'd assaulted
an officer.
inside the baptist church
the holy man talked
about us gay people
eating shit
yum.
the cops protected the door
from crazy blue-haired matt
who nearly put his fist
through the glass
screaming: *nazis!*
he was really upset.
at the idea of eating shit
so we stood in the street

and made the cops really mad.
peter called the cops once.
we knew these guys
were going to beat the crap
out of some gay person.
they slammed into jay
and waited,
perfectly poised
on the brink of some
enormous violence.
this dyke cop
with, you know, the hair
plunged into the guys' pockets
came up waving
brass knuckles
and a meat cleaver.
meat cleavers
are for chopping
big dead animals,
right through bone and
everything
so i guess it's good
that peter called the cops
but i couldn't do it.
the dyke cop
swinging the meat cleaver
yelling
*and what do we have*
*here?*

usually you find them
in other places.
protecting the christian's
big signs, red as hell,
talking about the things
gay people do
besides of course
eat shit.
market street on gay day
when they hang the rainbow flags

up and down the poles
making me in my pms cry
to feel so loved
by my city.
the gay police officers march.
are they relieved
that they don't have to protect
the christians
are they allowed
to have opinions
did they have to apply
for the day off
or did they just get it
because they're gay
and the city shut down
in their honor.

i have heard the dykes are the worst.
jen crying in her cell on gay day
for riding her bike
down a blocked off one way
street. i'm serious.
in the slammer.
they tried to rip the silver
from her nose
with some horrible tool
gave up and put her back
in her cage
and the dyke cops sang
*oh look she's cryyy-iiing*
how dare they
have they any idea
how awful
their hair is
and how so many people
hope that they die
on the street, shot
by someone
just like them.

## PASTRY TRAGEDY

let me tell you about this.
you left the bar
like you always do
like the bulb burning out the film
in the middle of the movie
the flick flick flick of the reel,
slap of tape,
and the audience in my ribs
roared, flung popcorn
and marched out.
home for a cry on the floor,
all spread out
the way you can spread out
on your own dusty floor,
tears and beers and music
carefully selected
to augment and encourage
my tragedy.
people came home
and i walked down the hall
with water dripping from my face
and sat quite pathetically
on the edge of the tub
in the dark, dead light bulb
and the girls in their underwear
brushed their teeth, spit foam
into the darkness
flung an arm around my shoulder
came into my room to my tragic
floor, bringing beer and smoking,
i changed the music, painted my nails,
one of the girls put on a wig and
bunny ears, lipstick, she preened
and i felt better, But I Will Never
Sleep, i wailed, I Will Never
i will never stop wanting
something impossibly
enormous, a parade of elephants

all decked out and marching
up my hall, I Will Never Be Happy Again o no
they brought me a brownie,
green to make me sleep
some puffy mold but
just don't eat that.
i gagged it down, drank
beer smoked got dizzy
laid in my bed giggled
ate more read tarot cards
o i know everything
in the church of 4am heartache
Go To Bed the girls said
and i did, to wake at 8
to begin my modeling career
the room swam like
something hot and liquid
a water snake swimming
it moved with me as i
walked my pumpkin head
down the hall
and collapsed at the toilet
and screamed
for the girls to come back
and save me
and wetness was just springing
from the meat of my body
i was hot as pavement
with my fist down my throat
shivering, the swimming world
of hallways and rooms,
alarmed roommates
climbing from beds
with cups of water that taste
like nothing and the call
to the poison control center,
Put Her To Bed,
there goes my modeling career
just like that, another drug tragedy
but not even, it's just a plant

really so embarrassing
to be knocked out naked and moaning
on the bathroom floor that's just
so scuzzy, from a bunch of leaves.
i got carried back to bed,
the legs wouldn't work
i thought about death
which seemed to be sleeping
beneath my pillow
poison control promised
i would live
i would miss so many things
if i died right now
but i suppose that's always the case.
i live.
stoned all day,
wandering the streets
with all the other half-dead,
keep going, i just
keep going

## ACKNOWLEDGMENTS

Thanks to Ali Liebegott for being such a total fucking inspiration. To Sash Sunday for patiently allowing me to torture her with poems about sea animals while drunk. Thanks to Eileen Myles for being such a spectacular example of all that is good. To Sara Seinberg and Tara Jepsen for being role models for art and friendship. To Kathleen Tomasik, the best sister in the whole world. To Jen Joseph for publishing these pieces. And thanks to Rocco for becoming, amazingly, both more lovable and more sexy every day. Thanks to Clint Catalyst for his high-octane fabulousness. I want to thank everyone who was around me during the years I was writing these poems, but the list would be ridiculous. Thanks, though.

Some of these poems first appeared in slightly different form in the following publications: *The City at the End of the World* (pure tragedy press), *heartbreak cigarettes* (borrowed time press), *oppress me before i kill again* (borrowed time press), *Tripping on Labia* (Mass Extinction Press), *Beyond Definition: New Writing from Gay and Lesbian San Francisco* (Manic D Press), *Signs of Life: Channelsurfing through 90's Culture* (Manic D Press), *As If* magazine and *Other* magazine. "The Beautiful" was included on *Greatest Spits* (Mr. Lady Records).